BAO

BAO

ASIAN-STYLE BUNS, DUMPLINGS & MORE
FROM YOUR BAMBOO STEAMER

with recipes by
LORETTA LIU

with photography by **CLARE WINFIELD**

RYLAND PETERS & SMALL
LONDON • NEW YORK

Senior Designer Megan Smith
Creative Director Leslie Harrington
Editor Kate Reeves-Brown
Editorial Director Julia Charles
Head of Production Patricia Harrington

Food Stylist Flossy McAslan
Prop Stylists Max Robinson & Lauren Miller
Indexer Hilary Bird

Published in 2022
by Ryland Peters & Small
20–21 Jockey's Fields
London WC1R 4BW
and
341 E 116th St
New York NY 10029
www.rylandpeters.com

Text © copyright Loretta Liu, Fiona
Smith, Vatcharin Bhumichitr and
Ryland Peters & Small 2022. Design
and photography © copyright Ryland
Peters & Small 2016, 2022. See full
credits on page 160.

ISBN: 978-1-78879-474-9

10 9 8 7 6 5 4 3 2 1

Printed and bound in China.

CIP data from the Library of
Congress has been applied for.

A CIP record for this book is
available from the British
Library.

NOTES

• Both British (Metric ml) and
American (Imperial oz. plus
US cup) measurements are
included in these recipes for
your convenience; however it is
important to work with one set
of measurements only and not
alternate between the two within
a recipe.

• All spoon measurements are
level unless otherwise specified.
A teaspoon is 5 ml, a tablespoon
is 15 ml.

• All eggs are medium (UK) or
large (US), unless specified as
large, in which case US extra-
large should be used. Uncooked
or partially cooked eggs should
not be served to the very old,
frail, young children, pregnant
women or those with
compromised immune systems.

• Steaming is not a precise form
of cooking. The cooking times in
these recipes are to be used as a
guideline. How long a dish takes
to cook at home will depend on
how your steamer basket has
been set up and the heat source.
If a recipe seems to be taking
longer than expected to cook,
be patient with it and allow it
to cook in its own time.

• Caution: Take care when
cooking as both steam
and water can reach high
temperatures. Do not leave
a steamer unattended and take
safety precautions around small
children. Neither the authors
nor the publisher can accept
liability for any accident or
incident resulting from cooking
the recipes in this book.

FSC
www.fsc.org

MIX
Paper | Supporting
responsible forestry
FSC® C008047

CONTENTS

INTRODUCTION TO STEAMING

Steaming is a healthy and efficient way to cook that retains all the freshness and goodness of food, without losing out on nutrients. It's especially good for delicate foods, such as fish, seafood and chicken, and really comes into its own with vegetables. From perfectly fluffy rice to delicate dumplings, this book provides everything you need to go full steam ahead.

TYPES OF STEAMER

A steamer is an essential for these recipes, but is also a handy tool to have in your kitchen. Steamers are inexpensive and relatively easy to come by. Some saucepan sets come with a steamer insert, but if you don't have one of these, bamboo steamers are both beautiful and inexpensive, as well as being readily available from most kitchen shops and Asian markets. Great results can be achieved from steaming with a bamboo basket over a (preferably cast-iron) wok, replenishing the water regularly as it boils. Alternatively, you can use a saucepan that fits the steamer basket on top, to prevent steam escaping from the sides. A purpose-made tiered steel steamer is a good choice, as is utilizing a fish kettle with a rack to separate the dish from the water. Electric steamers are another useful option, if you use this method of cooking regularly enough to warrant the investment.

SETTING UP YOUR STEAMER

A good rule of thumb for steaming is that the stronger the heat, the faster the dish will cook. Boiling a larger quantity of water will create more steam, which will cook the dish more rapidly. Whilst some of the recipes in this book, such as eggs, will cook best over a medium heat, a huge advantage of steaming is that dishes will not burn easily. As long as there is water in the base of the pan, you won't have to worry about burning; the dish will continue to cook over the steam.

With this in mind, the cooking times in these recipes are to be used as a guideline. How long a dish takes to cook will really depend on how your steamer basket has been set up. If a recipe seems to be taking longer than expected to cook, be patient with it and allow the dish to finish in its own time. Don't feel the need to rush the process and take these recipes as an opportunity to learn the art of steaming and enjoy the flavoursome foods that it can produce.

BASIC DOUGH RECIPES

There are five basic dough recipes used in this book. The bread dough and fluffy bread dough are used to create filled steamed buns and clamshell bao, the rice flour dough is used for filled dumplings, the crystal skin dough to make beautiful almost-translucent dumplings, and the egg dough for golden-coloured dim sum.

BREAD DOUGH

2 teaspoons easy-bake/
   rapid-rise dried yeast
450 g/3½ cups Asian white
   wheat flour
100 g/¾ cup plus 1 tablespoon
   icing/confectioners' sugar,
   sifted
15 g/2 tablespoons dried milk
   powder
¼ teaspoon salt
2 teaspoons baking powder
50 ml/3½ tablespoons
   vegetable oil, plus extra for
   oiling the bowl

MAKES 16 SKINS

Place the yeast in a large mixing bowl, then add the flour, sugar, milk powder, salt and baking powder. Make sure the yeast is separated from the salt by the layer of flour. Add the oil and 180 ml/¾ cup water and bring together with a dough scraper. When no dry flour remains, remove the dough from the bowl and place on a lightly floured surface. Knead firmly for 5–10 minutes, until smooth and elastic.

Lightly oil the mixing bowl. Shape the dough into two cylinders and place back in the oiled bowl, cover with oiled clingfilm/plastic wrap and leave in a warm place to rise for 40–60 minutes, or until doubled in size.

Remove the risen dough from the bowl, punch it down and knead it again briefly, but very carefully rather than firmly this time.

DOUGH ADDITIONS

» Add 30 g/1 oz. Korean chilli flakes/hot red pepper flakes with the flour.

» Add 5 g/⅙ oz. matcha powder with the flour.

» Add 2 teaspoons Chinese five-spice powder with the flour.

» Add a small pinch of Szechuan pepper with the flour.

» Add 5 g/⅙ oz. charcoal powder with the flour.

» Add 1 tablespoon squid ink into the water.

EGG DOUGH

150 g/1 cup plus 2 tablespoons Asian white
    wheat flour, plus extra for dusting
1 egg

MAKES 16 SKINS

Place the flour in a large mixing bowl and add
the egg and 40 ml/scant 3 tablespoons water.
Bring the mixture together, then turn the dough
out onto a lightly floured surface. Using lightly
floured hands, knead for 20–25 minutes. The
dough will be sticky at first but should become
smooth and silky.

Separate the dough in half and roll into two
equal cylinders, about 2.5 cm/1 in. in diameter.

Cover with a damp kitchen cloth to prevent it
from drying out and set aside to rest for
30 minutes.

CRYSTAL SKIN DOUGH

100 g/¾ cup wheat starch
50 g/½ cup tapioca starch
150 ml/⅔ cup boiling (not hot) water
salt
flour, for dusting

MAKES 16 SKINS

In a large mixing bowl, combine the wheat
starch, tapioca starch and a pinch of salt. Add
the boiling water and mix with a wooden spoon
until a dough is formed.

Transfer to a lightly floured surface and knead
until smooth. Separate the dough in half and
roll into two equal cylinders, about 2.5 cm/1 in.
in diameter.

Wrap in clingfilm/plastic wrap and let it rest
until needed.

FLUFFY BREAD DOUGH

230 g/1¾ cups plain/all-purpose flour
3 teaspoons baking powder
2 tablespoons caster/superfine sugar
80 ml/⅓ cup milk
3 tablespoons groundnut/peanut oil
salt
flour, for dusting

MAKES 24 SKINS

Put the flour in a large bowl and mix in the baking powder, sugar and ½ teaspoon salt. Stir in the milk, oil and 70 ml/¼ cup plus 2 teaspoons water to form a dough.

Turn the dough onto a floured board and knead for 5 minutes until it becomes elastic.

Cover with clingfilm/plastic wrap and let it rest at room temperature for 1 hour.

RICE FLOUR DOUGH

175 g/1⅓ cups plain/all-purpose flour,
    plus extra for dusting
125 g/1 cup minus 1 tablespoon rice flour
250 ml/1 cup boiling (not hot) water
2 tablespoons groundnut/peanut oil

MAKES 32 SKINS

Mix the two flours in a bowl, then stir in the boiling water and the oil. Stir until cool enough to handle, then knead to form a smooth mass.

Put in a plastic bag or wrap in clingfilm/plastic wrap and chill for 30 minutes.

BAO & STEAMED BUNS

CLAMSHELL BAO WITH KOREAN CABBAGE SLAW & SEARED BEEF

The Korean slaw, or kimchi, needs to be made a day in advance. Prepare it at the same time as the beef, which also needs to marinate in the fridge for 24 hours.

1 batch Bread Dough (see page 8), but add 30 g/1 oz. Korean chilli flakes/hot red pepper flakes with the flour

KOREAN CABBAGE SLAW
400 g/14 oz. white cabbage
1 brown onion
1 red onion
1 yellow (bell) pepper
2 carrots, peeled
100 g/3½ oz. Chinese chives
2 tablespoons Korean anchovy sauce
2 tablespoons Korean apple vinegar
50 g/½ cup Korean chilli flakes/ hot pepper flakes
50 g/scant ¼ cup clear honey
freshly squeezed juice of 2 limes

MARINATED BEEF
400 g/14 oz. beef fillet/ tenderloin
3 tablespoons light soy sauce
2 tablespoons clear honey
2 tablespoons mirin (Japanese rice wine)
2 tablespoons crushed/minced garlic
1 tablespoon sesame oil
4 tablespoons grated skinless pear
1 tablespoon ground white pepper
2 tablespoons sunflower or vegetable oil
100 g/¾ cup sesame seeds

MAKES 10

For the slaw, julienne the cabbage, onions, (bell) pepper and carrots into thin strips. Cut the Chinese chives into 5-cm/2-in. lengths. Place into a bowl and add the remaining slaw ingredients. Mix well, cover and place in the fridge to pickle for at least 24 hours.

For the marinated beef, slice the beef into thick slices. Place it into a bowl and add the soy sauce, clear honey, mirin (Japanese rice wine), crushed/ minced garlic, sesame oil, grated skinless pear, white pepper and 125 ml/ ½ cup water. Cover and place in the fridge for 24 hours.

Remove the beef from the fridge. Heat the oil in a frying pan/skillet over a medium heat and fry the beef slices until brown. Add the sesame seeds to finish, then remove from the pan. Divide beef into ten portions and set aside.

Cut some parchment paper into ten rectangles, 7 x 4 cm/2¾ x 1½ in. in size. Divide the bread dough into ten portions. Roll out each portion of dough into an oval shape about 1 cm/½ in. thick, then fold in half, placing a parchment rectangle in-between the folded dough.

Cut another ten squares of parchment paper just larger than the buns. Place a bun on each square, on its side, then place them into the steamer basket at least 5 cm/2 in. apart. You may have to do this in batches depending on the size of your steamer. Cover with oiled clingfilm/plastic wrap and leave to rise for 15 minutes.

Steam over boiling water for 10 minutes until the buns are light and fluffy. Allow to cool before serving.

To serve, place a little cabbage slaw into each bun, then top with a portion of beef filling.

BARBECUE PORK STEAMED BUNS

The pillowy-soft bread bun surrounding sweet and sticky char siu-style pork is just a heavenly combination. Traditionally, the filling for this type of steamed bun uses up leftovers from dinner the night before, but you can make the filling using fresh pork, as here.

**1 batch Bread Dough
(see page 8)**

FILLING
**1 tablespoon sunflower
or vegetable oil
1 shallot, chopped
2 tablespoons dry sherry
350 g/12 oz. pork loin, diced
1 teaspoon crushed/minced
garlic
2 tablespoons clear honey
2 tablespoons hoisin sauce
1 teaspoon Chinese five-spice
powder
1 tablespoon light soy sauce**

MAKES 16

To make the filling, heat the oil in a pan over a medium heat and add the shallot. Cook over a medium heat until softened and lightly caramelized, about 5–7 minutes. Pour in the sherry and let the alcohol cook out for a few minutes. Lower the heat a little and add the pork. Cook, stirring, for a further 2 minutes or until lightly browned.

Meanwhile, in a separate bowl, mix the garlic, honey, hoisin sauce, Chinese five-spice powder and soy sauce with 2 tablespoons water. Add this to the pork and shallot mixture. Stir well. Cover and cook over a low heat for 1 hour, or until the sauce has thickened and the pork is tender. Check occasionally during cooking to ensure the sauce does not dry out. Add a little extra water if necessary.

Divide the bread dough into 16 portions and roll out each dough ball to 7.5 cm/3 in. in diameter (try to make the centre slightly thicker than the edges so that it can hold the filling). Cover each dough circle with a damp kitchen cloth as you finish to stop it from drying out.

Allow the pork mixture to cool and finely chop the meat.

Place a heaped tablespoon of the filling in the centre of each dough circle. Gather the edges to form pleats and pinch to seal the top of the bun.

Cut out 16 squares of parchment paper just larger than the buns. Place a bun on each square of parchment and then place into the steamer basket at least 5 cm/2 in. apart. You may have to do this in batches depending on the size of your steamer. Cover with oiled clingfilm/plastic wrap and allow to rise for 30 minutes.

Steam over boiling water for 8–10 minutes until the dough is light and fluffy. Allow to cool slightly, then serve.

CLAMSHELL BAO WITH CUCUMBER & MINT SLAW & CRISPY TOFU/BEANCURD

Here, tofu/beancurd is uplifted by a vibrant, crunchy slaw made from cucumber, mint and (bell) pepper. The zingy lime juice and the garlic chives really pack a punch.

1 batch Bread Dough (see page 8), but add 5 g/⅙ oz. matcha powder into the flour

CUCUMBER & MINT SLAW
4 long cucumbers
100 g/3½ oz. garlic chives
1 yellow (bell) pepper
100 g/3½ oz. fresh mint
2 tablespoons Korean anchovy sauce
2 tablespoons chopped garlic
2 tablespoons ground ginger
60 g/generous ¼ cup clear honey, or to taste
freshly squeezed juice of 3 limes
100 g/¾ cup sunflower seeds
salt

CRISPY TOFU/BEANCURD
150 g/5¼ oz. firm tofu/beancurd steaks
2 tablespoons sunflower or vegetable oil
100 g/¾ cup sesame seeds (optional)

MAKES 10

Start by making the cucumber and mint slaw. Remove the cucumber seeds and julienne the cucumber into matchsticks, about 5 cm/2 in. long. Sprinkle 1 tablespoon salt evenly all over the cucumber pieces and leave them to rest for 30 minutes. Strain the water from the cucumber and pat dry with paper towels.

Cut the garlic chives and (bell) pepper into 5-cm/2-in. lengths and add to the cucumber. Pick the mint leaves from the stems and add to the cucumber mix. Add the remaining slaw ingredients, mix well, cover and place in the fridge for at least 2 hours.

Dry the tofu/beancurd steaks with paper towels. Heat the oil in a frying pan/skillet over a medium heat and fry the tofu/beancurd steaks until coloured. Add the sesame seeds, if using, to finish, then remove from the pan. Slice into ten portions.

Cut some parchment paper into ten rectangles, 7 x 4 cm/2¾ x 1½ in. in size. Divide the bread dough into ten portions. Roll out each portion of dough into an oval shape about 1 cm/½ in. thick, then fold in half, placing a parchment rectangle in-between the folded dough.

Cut another ten squares of parchment paper just larger than the buns. Place a bun on each square, on its side, then place them into the steamer basket at least 5 cm/2 in. apart. You may have to do this in batches depending on the size of your steamer. Cover with oiled clingfilm/plastic wrap and leave to rise for 15 minutes.

Steam over boiling water for 10 minutes until the buns are light and fluffy. Allow to cool before serving.

To serve, place some cucumber and mint slaw into each bun and top with a portion of tofu/beancurd steak.

CLAMSHELL BAO WITH ROAST DUCK & HOISIN SAUCE

Duck and hoisin sauce is one of the most popular pairings in Chinese cuisine. Add crunchy cucumber, spring onions/scallions and coriander/cilantro leaves for the perfect finish.

1 batch Bread Dough (see page 8), but replace 90 g/ 2/3 cup Asian white wheat flour with Asian wholemeal wheat flour (add 15% more water if using regular wholemeal flour) and add 2 teaspoons Chinese five-spice powder

ROAST DUCK
4 duck breasts
2 teaspoons Chinese five-spice powder
100 g/3½ oz. maltrose/malt syrup (very important)
2 tablespoons dark soy sauce
salt and freshly ground black pepper

TO SERVE
1 cucumber
2 spring onions/scallions
100 g/3½ oz. Chinese coriander/cilantro
10 tablespoons hoisin sauce

MAKES 10

For the roast duck, season the duck breasts with the Chinese five-spice powder and 1 teaspoon each of salt and pepper.

Heat 1 litre/4 cups water in a pan with the maltrose/malt syrup and dark soy sauce. Using a ladle , give the duck breast skins a rinse over twice (only the skin side) with the hot liquid. Then leave the duck breasts to dry, skin-side up, for at least 6 hours in a cool room or under a low fan.

After 6 hours, preheat the oven to 180°C (350°F) Gas 4.

Roast the duck breasts in the preheated oven for 15–20 minutes until cooked to your liking. Allow to cool, then slice into ten even slices.

Cut some parchment paper into ten rectangles, 7 x 4 cm/2¾ x 1½ in. in size. Divide the bread dough into ten portions. Roll out each portion of dough into an oval shape about 1 cm/½ in. thick, then fold in half, placing a parchment rectangle in-between the folded dough.

Cut another ten squares of parchment paper just larger than the buns. Place a bun on each square, on its side, then place them into the steamer basket at least 5 cm/2 in. apart. You may have to do this in batches depending on the size of your steamer. Cover with oiled clingfilm/plastic wrap and leave to rise for 15 minutes.

Steam over boiling water for 10 minutes until the buns are light and fluffy. Allow to cool before serving.

Remove the cucumber seeds and julienne the cucumber into thin strips (about 1 cm/½ in. thick and 6 cm/2½ in. long). Thinly slice the spring onions/scallions and soak them in cold water to refresh. Pick the coriander/cilantro leaves from the stems and soak in cold water to refresh. Strain the leaves to dry.

To serve, smear a tablespoon of hoisin sauce into each bun and add some cucumber, spring onion/scallion and coriander/cilantro. Top with a slice of duck breast and serve.

LITTLE SZECHUAN CHICKEN STEAMED BUNS

Traditionally filled with pork or bean paste, these fluffy buns are a popular and comforting dim sum option. For a whiter bun, you can replace half the flour with potato flour, but the dough is less elastic, so harder to handle.

1 batch Fluffy Bread Dough
(see page 11)

FILLING
4 chicken thighs
3 tablespoons dark soy sauce
2 tablespoons clear honey
1 tablespoon Shaoxing (Chinese rice wine) or dry sherry
1–2 tablespoons hot chilli/chili sauce
2–3 garlic cloves, crushed/minced
1 tablespoon Szechuan peppercorns, crushed

MAKES 24

Put the chicken in a baking dish. Put the soy sauce in a bowl, mix in the honey, Shaoxing or sherry, chilli/chili sauce, garlic and peppercorns, add to the chicken and turn to coat. Cover with foil or a lid and place in the fridge to marinate for 30 minutes–2 hours.

Preheat the oven to 180°C (350°F) Gas 4.

Transfer the baking dish, still covered, to the preheated oven and roast for 20 minutes, then uncover and cook a further 20 minutes until cooked through. Let cool, then remove the meat from the bones, shred it finely and mix the shredded meat with any marinade and juices left in the dish.

Divide the dough into 24 pieces and cover with a damp cloth. Take each piece of dough and, using your fingers, shape into a 6-cm/2½-in. disc. Put a teaspoon of the chicken filling in the centre of each one and gather up the dough around it. Pinch the edges together and twist to seal.

Place the buns, sealed edges up, on a sheet of parchment that will fit in your steamer, or on 24 individual parchment squares, then place them into the steamer basket at least 2.5 cm/1 in. apart. You may have to do this in batches depending on the size of your steamer.

Steam over boiling water for 15–20 minutes until the buns are light and fluffy. Allow to cool slightly, then serve.

CLAMSHELL BAO WITH MISO SALMON

Delicate salmon marinated in miso, mirin, sake and honey makes the perfect filling for these soft clamshell buns. Add some crunchy leaves, some creamy, ripe avocado and some fresh red onion slices, and you have a match made in bao heaven.

1 batch Bread Dough (see page 8), but replace Asian white wheat flour with Asian wholemeal wheat flour (add 15% more water if using regular wholemeal flour)

MISO SALMON

10 portions salmon fillet, about 6 cm/2½ in. in length
1 tablespoon miso paste
1 tablespoon mirin (Japanese rice wine)
1 tablespoon cooking sake (Chinese cooking rice wine)
1 tablespoon clear honey
1 tablespoon ground black pepper

TO SERVE

4 ripe avocados, pitted and peeled
10 Little Gem/Bibb lettuce leaves
1 small red onion, sliced

MAKES 10

Place the salmon portions into a casserole with the other miso salmon ingredients and 125 ml/½ cup water. Mix well, cover and place in the fridge for at least 4 hours to marinate.

When ready to cook, preheat the oven to 180°C (350°F) Gas 4.

Remove the lid or cover from the casserole and cook the fish in the preheated oven for 15 minutes until cooked through (reduce the oven temperature slightly if the salmon is browning too much). Allow to cool while you prepare the buns.

Cut some parchment paper into ten rectangles, 7 x 4 cm/2¾ x 1½ in. in size. Divide the bread dough into ten portions. Roll out each portion of dough into an oval shape about 1 cm/½ in. thick, then fold in half, placing a parchment rectangle in-between the folded dough.

Cut another ten squares of parchment paper just larger than the buns. Place a bun on each square, on its side, then place them into the steamer basket at least 5 cm/2 in. apart. You may have to do this in batches depending on the size of your steamer. Cover with oiled clingfilm/plastic wrap and leave to rise for 15 minutes.

Steam over boiling water for 10 minutes until the buns are light and fluffy. Allow to cool before serving.

Slice the avocados and divide into ten portions.

To serve, place a lettuce leaf, avocado portion and a few red onion slices into each bun and top with the miso salmon.

CLAMSHELL BAO WITH CHINESE VEGETABLES

The fashionable clamshell shape of these buns shows off the vibrant colours of the vegetables. Take care with preparation as your knife skills will be on show!

1 batch Bread Dough
   (see page 8)
1 head Chinese cabbage,
   leaves separated
3 handfuls Chinese spinach
2 small leeks
2 tablespoons sunflower oil
1 carrot, peeled and grated
8 oyster mushrooms, sliced
3 Chinese chive stalks, white
   parts removed, sliced

a large handful fresh coriander/
   cilantro, finely chopped
vegetarian stir-fry sauce,
   to serve

MAKES 10

Cut some parchment paper into ten rectangles, 7 x 4 cm/2¾ x 1½ in. in size. Divide the bread dough into ten portions. Roll out each portion of dough into an oval shape about 1 cm/½ in. thick, then fold in half, placing a parchment rectangle in-between the folded dough.

Cut another ten squares of parchment paper just larger than the buns. Place a bun on each square, on its side, then place them into the steamer basket at least 5 cm/2 in. apart. You may have to do this in batches depending on the size of your steamer. Cover with oiled clingfilm/plastic wrap and leave to rise for 15 minutes.

While the buns are rising, slice the cabbage leaves, spinach and leeks lengthwise into ribbons approximately 6 cm/2¼ in. long. Set aside.

Steam the buns over boiling water for 10 minutes until light and fluffy. Allow to cool before serving.

Heat the sunflower oil in a wok and stir-fry all the vegetables and coriander/cilantro for around 2–3 minutes. Add vegetarian stir-fry sauce to taste and give the vegetables a quick toss.

To serve, fill the buns with the hot vegetables and serve at once.

FRIED PRAWN/SHRIMP & SCALLOP STEAMED BUNS

These buns are intensely delicious, yet classy comfort food. With the surprise of a whole scallop in the centre, they are sure to be a winner. Separate dipping sauces are not usually needed with buns such as these, as the filling inside should be juicy enough.

1 batch Bread Dough
(see page 8)

FILLING
2 spring onions/scallions,
chopped
¼ head cabbage, chopped
400 g/14 oz. raw prawns/shrimp,
peeled and deveined
3 tablespoons oyster sauce
2 tablespoons Korean chilli
flakes/hot pepper flakes
1 tablespoon sesame oil
2 tablespoons Shaoxing
(Chinese rice wine) or
dry sherry
16 scallops

MAKES 16

To make the filling, mix the spring onions/scallions and cabbage together in a large bowl. Mince the prawns/shrimp by chopping them very finely with a sharp knife. Add these to the vegetables, along with the oyster sauce, chilli flakes/hot pepper flakes, sesame oil and Shaoxing or sherry. Mix together well and chill in the fridge.

Divide the bread dough into 16 portions and roll out each dough ball to 7.5 cm/3 in. in diameter (try to make the centre slightly thicker than the edges so that it can hold the filling). Cover each dough circle with a damp kitchen cloth as you finish to stop it from drying out.

Place a tablespoon of the prawn/shrimp filling in the centre of each dough circle and place a scallop on top. Gather the edges to form pleats and pinch to seal the top of the bun.

Cut out 16 squares of parchment paper just larger than the buns. Place a bun on each square of parchment and then place into the steamer basket at least 5 cm/2 in. apart. You may have to do this in batches depending on the size of your steamer. Cover with oiled clingfilm/plastic wrap and allow to rise for 30 minutes.

Steam over boiling water for 8–10 minutes until the dough is light and fluffy. Allow to cool slightly, then serve.

CHAR SIU STEAMED BUNS

If you live near a Chinatown market, you can buy their delicious barbecued pork, char siu.
If you don't, try the home-style version given below, reserving a little for the buns.

½ batch Fluffy Bread Dough
   (see page 11)

FILLING
1 tablespoon groundnut/peanut
   oil
1 tablespoon chopped onion
1 garlic clove, crushed/minced
125 g/4 oz. Chinese barbecued
   pork (char siu), finely chopped
   (see below)
2 spring onions/scallions,
   chopped, plus extra to serve
   (optional)
1 tablespoon light soy sauce
freshly ground black pepper
½ teaspoon sugar
¼ teaspoon sesame oil

MAKES 8

Heat the oil in a wok over a high heat, add the onion and garlic and stir-fry until golden. Add the pork, spring onions/scallions, soy sauce, pepper, sugar and sesame oil, stir-fry quickly over a high heat, then reduce the heat and simmer gently for about 5 minutes. Let cool.

Turn out the dough onto a work surface and knead for 5 minutes. Divide into eight portions, then roll each piece into a ball and flatten to a disc.

Put one-eighth of the filling in the middle of each disc, then gradually work the outside edge of the disc around and over the top to enclose the filling. Seal.

Cut out eight squares of parchment paper, about 10-cm/4-in. square. Place a bun on each square of parchment and then place into the steamer basket at least 5 cm/2 in. apart. You may have to do this in batches depending on the size of your steamer.

Steam over simmering water for about 30 minutes, until well puffed. Allow to cool slightly, then serve with some extra chopped spring onions/scallions, if you like.

CHINESE BARBECUE PORK

Cut 1 kg/2 lb. 4 oz. pork fillet/tenderloin into two long strips lengthways. Rub with 1 tablespoon black pepper and 1 tablespoon Chinese five-spice powder. Put 4 tablespoons soy sauce into a shallow dish and stir in 2 teaspoons sesame oil.

Add the pork and turn to coat well. Cover and chill overnight to develop the flavours. Next day, let return to room temperature for 1 hour, then cook on a barbecue/outdoor grill or roast on a rack in a preheated oven at 200°C (400°F) Gas 6 for about 15 minutes. Reduce the heat to 180°C (350°F) Gas 4 and continue roasting for about 20 minutes. Let rest for 20 minutes before cutting.

CLAMSHELL BAO WITH CHICKEN TERIYAKI

The chicken teriyaki is best when left to marinate in the fridge for 48 hours,
so you need to start this recipe 2 days before you plan to cook it.

1 batch Bread Dough
   (see page 8)

CHICKEN TERIYAKI
5 chicken breasts or boneless
   chicken thighs
1 tablespoon dark soy sauce
1 tablespoon mirin
   (Japanese rice wine)
1 tablespoon cooking sake
   (Chinese cooking rice wine)
2 tablespoons soy sauce
2 tablespoons clear honey
3 garlic cloves, chopped
salt and freshly ground black
   pepper

TO SERVE
10 Little Gem/Bibb lettuce
   leaves
20 tomato slices
shredded spring onions/
   scallions

MAKES 10

Slice the chicken breasts or thighs across the grain into ten slices in total, then place into a casserole with all the other chicken teriyaki ingredients, 1 teaspoon salt, 1 tablespoon ground black pepper and 125 ml/½ cup water. Mix well, cover and place in the fridge to marinate for 48 hours.

When ready to cook, preheat the oven to 190°C (375°F) Gas 5.

Remove the lid or cover from the chicken and roast in the preheated oven for 20 minutes until cooked through (reduce the oven temperature slightly if the chicken is browning too much). Allow to cool.

Cut some parchment paper into ten rectangles, 7 x 4 cm/2¾ x 1½ in. in size. Divide the bread dough into ten portions. Roll out each portion of dough into an oval shape about 1 cm/½ in. thick, then fold in half, placing a parchment rectangle in-between the folded dough.

Cut another ten squares of parchment paper just larger than the buns. Place a bun on each square, on its side, then place them into the steamer basket at least 5 cm/2 in. apart. You may have to do this in batches depending on the size of your steamer. Cover with oiled clingfilm/plastic wrap and leave to rise for 15 minutes.

Steam over boiling water for 10 minutes until the buns are light and fluffy. Allow to cool before serving.

To serve, place one lettuce leaf and two slices of tomato into each bun, then add a piece of chicken and some shredded spring onions/scallions.

STEAMED BUNS FILLED WITH SPICY MALA LAMB & MINT

This Szechuan-inspired minced/ground lamb filling is rich with warming cumin, ground coriander and Szechuan pepper, which marries beautifully with the fragrant fresh mint.

1 batch Bread Dough (see page 8), but add 1 teaspoon ground Szechuan pepper with the flour

FILLING
200 g/7 oz. minced/ground lamb
1 leek, chopped
60 g/2 oz. preserved spicy mustard stems, chopped
3 garlic cloves, chopped
20 g/¾ oz. fresh ginger, peeled and chopped
2 long red chillies/chiles (deseeded if you don't want it too hot), chopped
60 g/2 oz. fresh mint leaves, thinly sliced
60 g/2 oz. courgette/zucchini, finely chopped
2 tablespoons light soy sauce
2 tablespoons Shaoxing (Chinese rice wine) or dry sherry
1 tablespoon ground cumin
2 teaspoons ground coriander
2 tablespoons groundnut/ peanut oil
1 tablespoon cornflour/ cornstarch
½ tablespoon ground Szechuan pepper, or to taste
salt

MAKES 16

Put the lamb into a bowl and add all the other filling ingredients and 2 teaspoons salt. Mix well, cover and place in the fridge to marinate for at least 2 hours.

Divide the bread dough into 16 portions and roll out each dough ball to 7.5 cm/3 in. in diameter (try to make the centre slightly thicker than the edges so that it can hold the filling). Cover each dough circle with a damp kitchen cloth as you finish to stop it from drying out.

Divide the lamb filling into 16 portions and place a portion into the centre of each dough circle. Gather the dough to form pleats and pinch to seal the top of the bun.

Cut out 16 squares of parchment paper just larger than the buns. Place a bun on each square of parchment and then place into the steamer basket at least 5 cm/2 in. apart. You may have to do this in batches depending on the size of your steamer. Cover with oiled clingfilm/plastic wrap and allow to rise for 30 minutes.

Steam over boiling water for 8–10 minutes until the dough is light and fluffy. Allow to cool slightly, then serve.

MOLTEN EGG CUSTARD BUNS

When you cut into these striking black buns, the yellow egg custard will dramatically ooze out. Charcoal powder is the secret ingredient added to the bread dough.

1 batch Bread Dough (see
  page 8), but add 5 g/⅙ oz.
  charcoal powder to the flour

FILLING
90 g/3 oz. salted egg yolks
125 g/9 tablespoons unsalted
  butter, melted
50 g/scant ½ cup custard
  powder/instant vanilla
  pudding
85 g/7 tablespoons sugar
60 g/¾ cup whole milk powder/
  dried milk
50 ml/3½ tablespoons full-fat/
  whole milk

MAKES 16

To make the molten egg filling, separate the salted egg yolks from the whites and wash the fresh salted egg yolk with water to remove the egg white membrane. Steam the salted yolks over high heat for 15 minutes, then turn off the heat and use the sides of a cleaver to mash the salted egg yolk to a fine crumb.

Put the crumbed egg yolks into a bowl with the rest of the filling ingredients and mix into a firm, round paste. Flatten the paste slightly, then wrap in clingfilm/plastic wrap and chill in fridge for 30 minutes, or until the paste hardens.

Remove the paste from the fridge and divide it into 16 portions. Roll them into balls and place back in the fridge again to harden while you prepare the buns.

Divide the bread dough into 16 portions and roll out each dough ball to 7.5 cm/3 in. in diameter (try to make the centre slightly thicker than the edges so that it can hold the filling). Cover each dough circle with a damp kitchen cloth as you finish to stop it from drying out.

Place a portion of filling into the centre of each dough circle. Place the dough on the palm of your hand and wrap the dough around the filling, then pinch the excess dough at the ends between your thumb and index fingers and seal the filled dough to form a ball.

Cut out 16 squares of parchment paper just larger than the buns. Place a bun on each square of parchment, seam-side down, and then place into the steamer basket at least 5 cm/2 in. apart. You may have to do this in batches depending on the size of your steamer. Cover with oiled clingfilm/plastic wrap and allow to rise for 10 minutes.

Steam over boiling water for 8 minutes until the dough is light and fluffy. Do not overcook the buns otherwise the buns will over-expand and burst. Allow to cool for 10 minutes, then serve.

STEAMED BUNS WITH CHICKEN & GARLIC CHIVES

You can use chicken breasts or thighs for the filling in these beautifully soft buns.
The scattering of roasted sesame seeds on top is a lovely finishing touch.

1 batch Bread Dough (see
  page 8), but add 1 tablespoon
  squid ink into the water

FILLING
200 g/7 oz. chicken breasts
  or boneless chicken thighs
100 g/3½ oz. garlic chives
50 g/1¾ oz. firm tofu/beancurd,
  finely chopped
2 tablespoons sunflower or
  vegetable oil
2 tablespoons light soy sauce
2 tablespoons sesame oil
1 teaspoon ground Szechuan
  pepper
1 teaspoon black vinegar or
  balsamic vinegar
2 teaspoons potato starch
130 g/1 cup roasted sesame
  seeds
salt

MAKES 16

For the filling, chop the chicken into small cubes and place in a bowl.

Cut the garlic chives into 1-cm/½-in. lengths and add into the bowl with the chicken, along with the finely chopped tofu/beancurd.

Place a wok over a medium heat, add the oil and then fry the chicken mixture quickly until just cooked. Add the soy sauce, sesame oil, Szechuan pepper and 2 teaspoons salt, then drizzle in the vinegar.

Mix the potato starch with 125 ml/½ cup water and then pour over the filling. Bring to the boil, and, just as it boils and thickens slightly, remove the filling from the wok. If the filling is sticky and dry, add extra water. Set aside to cool.

Divide the bread dough into 16 portions and roll out each dough ball to 7.5 cm/3 in. in diameter (try to make the centre slightly thicker than the edges so that it can hold the filling). Cover each dough circle with a damp kitchen cloth as you finish to stop it from drying out.

Put the roasted sesame seeds into a shallow dish.

Divide the chicken filling into 16 portions and place a portion into the centre of each dough circle. Gather the dough to form pleats and pinch to seal the top of the bun.

Using a pastry brush, lightly brush water on the top of each bun, then dip the top of each bun into the dish of sesame seeds.

Cut out 16 squares of parchment paper just larger than the buns. Place a bun on each square of parchment and then place into the steamer basket at least 5 cm/2 in. apart. You may have to do this in batches depending on the size of your steamer. Cover with oiled clingfilm/plastic wrap and allow to rise for 30 minutes.

Steam over boiling water for 8–10 minutes until the dough is light and fluffy. Allow to cool slightly, then serve.

RED CURRY CHICKEN & LENTIL STEAMED BUNS

Here is a taste of Thailand fused with traditional Chinese fluffy steamed buns
– use shop-bought Thai red curry paste to make the filling quick and easy.

1 batch Bread Dough
  (see page 8)

FILLING
2 tablespoons sunflower oil
2 onions, thinly sliced
2 garlic cloves, crushed/minced
1–2 tablespoons Thai red curry
  paste, to taste
2 chicken breasts, cut into
  bite-size pieces
500 ml/2 cups hot chicken stock
80 g/scant ½ cup dried red
  lentils

MAKES 16

For the filling, heat 1 tablespoon of the oil in a large frying pan/skillet and add the onions. Cook for 3 minutes over a gentle heat until soft and fragrant. Stir in the garlic and curry paste and cook for 1–2 minutes more.

Add the chicken pieces and cook for 2–3 minutes. Stir in the stock and lentils, bring to the boil, cover and simmer for 25 minutes, stirring occasionally, until the lentils are tender and the chicken is cooked. Set aside to cool.

Divide the bread dough into 16 portions and roll out each dough ball to 7.5 cm/3 in. in diameter (try to make the centre slightly thicker than the edges so that it can hold the filling). Cover each dough circle with a damp kitchen cloth as you finish to stop it from drying out.

Place a tablespoon of filling into the centre of each dough circle. Gather and pleat the edges, pinching to seal the top of the bun.

Cut out 16 squares of parchment paper just larger than the buns. Place a bun on each square of parchment, seam-side down, and then place into the steamer basket at least 5 cm/2 in. apart. You may have to do this in batches depending on the size of your steamer. Cover with oiled clingfilm/plastic wrap and allow to rise for 30 minutes.

Steam over boiling water for 15–20 minutes until the dough is light and fluffy. Allow to cool slightly, then serve.

DIM SUM & FILLED DUMPLINGS

DUMPLINGS WITH PEPPER SOY

The round dumpling wrappers for this variation on a Cantonese classic are available in the chilled sections of Chinese supermarkets. You can also use wonton wrappers, but they won't have the perfect, moon-white translucence of the real thing.

6 Chinese dried mushrooms

125 g/4 oz. cooked, peeled red prawns/shrimp

150 g/5¼ oz. smoked streaky/fatty bacon

125 g/4 oz. skinless chicken breast

1 tablespoon cornflour/cornstarch

1 tablespoon groundnut/peanut oil

10 water chestnuts, finely diced

1 tablespoon Shaoxing (Chinese rice wine) or dry sherry

1 teaspoon sugar

1 teaspoon sesame oil

1½ tablespoons dark soy sauce

3-cm/1¼-in. piece fresh ginger, peeled and grated

50 dumpling wrappers (2 packs)

50 fresh coriander/cilantro leaves

TO SERVE

1 tablespoon Japanese seven-spice (shichimi togarishi)

125 ml/½ cup dark soy sauce

MAKES 50

Put the mushrooms into a bowl and cover with boiling water for about 15 minutes to rehydrate. Drain and squeeze as dry as possible. Remove and discard the stems and any hard pieces. Chop the mushrooms finely and set aside.

Split the prawns/shrimp in half lengthways, then cut them into pieces about 2 cm/¾ in. long. Set aside.

Chop the bacon and chicken and transfer to a small food processor. Add the cornflour/cornstarch and blend to a paste.

Put the oil into a wok and heat well, swirling the oil around the surface of the wok. Add the chicken paste and stir-fry, breaking up any lumps, until opaque. Add the mushrooms, water chestnuts, Shaoxing or dry sherry, sugar, sesame oil, soy sauce and grated ginger. Stir-fry until heated through, to mix the flavours, then let cool and chill until ready to assemble.

When ready to assemble, working on 2–3 wrappers at a time and keeping the others covered, put 1 heaped teaspoon of the chicken mixture in the centre of a dumpling wrapper. Put a piece of prawn/shrimp, red-side out, on one side of the filling, and a coriander/cilantro leaf on the other side. Dip your finger in water and run it around the edge of the wrapper. Bring the edges of the wrapper together to form a half moon, then pleat the edges to form a crest. Tap the base of the moon on the work surface to flatten. Cover with a cloth until all the dumplings have been made.

Arrange in the steamer basket, making sure you leave space between the dumplings (cook in batches, if necessary).

Steam over boiling water for 9–10 minutes until done – the dough will become slightly translucent, letting the green coriander/cilantro and red prawn/shrimp show through.

To make the dipping sauce, stir the Japanese seven-spice into the soy. Serve the dumplings hot alongside the dipping sauce.

LOTUS LEAF RICE DUMPLINGS

The lotus is considered a sacred plant in Chinese culture, the fruit of which is delicious but hard to find. More prevalent are the giant strong-textured leaves, perfect for holding fillings, but still pleasant to eat.

370 g/2 cups sweet glutinous/ sticky rice
4 dried lotus leaves
1 teaspoon sesame oil
1 chicken breast, finely chopped
1 tablespoon cornflour/ cornstarch
2 teaspoons vegetable oil
4 shiitake mushrooms, sliced
1 leek, sliced
1 Chinese sausage (marinated and smoked pork sausage found in Chinese markets), thinly sliced
2 teaspoons oyster sauce
2 teaspoons soy sauce
1 tablespoon Shaoxing (Chinese rice wine) or dry sherry
2 tablespoons caster/superfine sugar
salt

a rice cooker

MAKES 8

Rinse and drain the rice, then soak in 600 ml/2½ cups water for 2 hours.

Meanwhile, cut each folded lotus leaf in half lengthways. Submerge the leaves in hot water and leave to soak for 30 minutes, pressing down if they float up. Trim the leaves with kitchen scissors/shears until they are a similar size and trim off the hard stalk end.

Drain the rice thoroughly. In the bowl of a rice cooker, place the rice, sesame oil, ½ teaspoon salt and 250 ml/1 cup water. Cook following the packet instructions.

Mix the chopped chicken with the cornflour/cornstarch. Put the vegetable oil in a large frying pan/skillet over a high heat and fry the chicken for 3 minutes. Add the mushrooms, sliced leek and sausage and cook, stirring for a further few minutes. Lower the heat and add the oyster sauce, soy sauce, Shaoxing or sherry and caster/superfine sugar. Stir-fry until the chicken is cooked and the vegetables are tender. Set aside to cool.

Divide the cooked rice into eight portions. With wet fingertips, divide each portion of rice in half. Shape eight half-portions into rectangles in the centre of each lotus leaf half. Put a tablespoon of chicken mixture on top and spread evenly. Top the meat with a second half-portion of rice to cover them completely.

Fold the leaves up over the rice. Fold in the left and right sides, and then roll each leaf away from you towards the curved edge to make a rectangular packet.

Place the dumplings seam-side down in the steamer basket, leaving space between them (cook in batches, if necessary).

Steam over boiling water for 45 minutes, or until heated through. Serve warm.

PRAWN/SHRIMP DUMPLINGS

Also known as har gao, these little dumplings are one of the most iconic dim sum dishes. The crystal skin should be delicate enough to just about see the pink prawns/shrimp peeping through.

1 batch Crystal Skin Dough
(see page 10)

FILLING
50 g/1¾ oz. firm tofu/beancurd,
drained and sliced
150 g/5¼ oz. raw prawns/
shrimp, peeled and deveined
1 teaspoon crushed/minced
fresh ginger
1 teaspoon crushed/minced
garlic
½ teaspoon Shaoxing (Chinese
rice wine) or dry sherry
½ teaspoon sugar
1 teaspoon olive oil
1 teaspoon cornflour/cornstarch
salt and ground white pepper

DIPPING SAUCE
1 small piece fresh ginger,
peeled and thinly sliced into
matchsticks
6 tablespoons black vinegar

MAKES 16

For the filling, squeeze out the excess water from the tofu/beancurd and very finely chop using a sharp knife.

Chop each prawn/shrimp into 4–5 small pieces and place in a bowl. Add the drained and chopped tofu, ginger, garlic, Shaoxing or dry sherry, sugar, oil, cornflour/cornstarch and ½ teaspoon each salt and ground white pepper. Mix well and set aside in the fridge to marinate while you make the dough.

Divide the crystal skin dough into 16 equal balls. On a lightly floured surface use a rolling pin to flatten the dough balls into thin discs, about 5 cm/2 in. in diameter. Cover the finished skins with a damp kitchen cloth as you work so that they don't dry out.

Place a large teaspoon of filling neatly into the centre of a skin. Fold the skin in half over the filling. Pinch one end together and start to crimp the edge by making small folds to form pleats to create the traditional crescent shape. Repeat with the remaining skins and filling.

Put the dumplings into the steamer basket lined with parchment paper, making sure there is space between them (cook in batches, if necessary).

Steam over boiling water for 15–20 minutes, or until the skins are transparent and the prawns/shrimp are red.

To make the dipping sauce, stir the sliced ginger into the black vinegar. Serve the dumplings hot alongside the dipping sauce.

DUMPLINGS WITH MAKRUT LIME & LEMONGRASS

South-east Asian flavours take centre stage in these pretty dumplings. They make perfect party food as they freeze well and look gorgeous served straight from bamboo steamers.

2 garlic cloves, crushed/minced

4-cm/1½-in. piece fresh galangal or ginger, peeled and finely chopped

2 stalks lemongrass, finely chopped

8 makrut lime leaves, finely chopped

2 hot Thai chillies/chiles, deseeded and finely chopped

12 shallots, finely chopped

4 tablespoons fish sauce or light soy sauce

500 g/1 lb. 2 oz. skinless, boneless chicken breast, minced/ground

4 tablespoons coconut cream

50 small fresh wonton wrappers (2 packs)

banana leaves, for steaming (optional)

sweet chilli/chili sauce, to serve

MAKES 50

Using a small food processor or large mortar and pestle, grind the garlic, galangal or ginger, lemongrass, makrut lime leaves, chillies/chiles and shallots to form a paste – add a little of the fish sauce or soy sauce if needed. Transfer to a bowl, add the remaining fish or soy sauce, minced chicken and coconut cream and stir well.

Cut the wonton wrappers into rounds and discard the trimmings – keep them covered with a kitchen cloth so they don't dry out. Line the bamboo steamer with banana leaves (or parchment paper).

Put a wrapper on a dry surface and spread with a teaspoon of filling. Gather up the edges to form a basket shape, leaving the middle exposed. Drop it gently onto the work surface to flatten the bottom and settle the filling. Place in the steamer. Repeat until all are made, keeping the wrappers and the dumplings covered as you go and leaving space between the dumplings (cook in batches, if necessary).

Steam over boiling water for 8 minutes and serve immediately with sweet chilli/chili sauce for dipping.

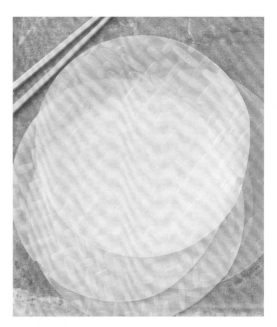

CRAB DUMPLINGS

These bite-size morsels are typical of Chinese dim sum – they look elegant, smell tantalizing and taste good! Use fresh crab meat for the very best flavour. If you do need to use frozen crab meat, make sure it is well drained before using.

125 g/4 oz. fresh crab meat
50 g/1¾ oz. cooked, peeled
   prawns/shrimp, chopped
4 canned water chestnuts,
   finely chopped
2 spring onions/scallions,
   finely chopped
2.5-cm/1-in. piece fresh ginger,
   peeled and grated
1 small chilli/chile, deseeded
   and finely chopped
1 tablespoon chopped fresh
   coriander/cilantro
1 tablespoon light soy sauce
20 x 8–9 cm/3½ in. round
   wonton wrappers
toasted sesame seeds,
   to garnish
dipping sauce of your choice,
   to serve

MAKES 20

In a bowl mix together the crab meat, prawns/shrimp, water chestnuts, spring onions/scallions, ginger, chilli/chile, coriander/cilantro and soy sauce.

Brush the edges of a wonton wrapper with water. Place a heaped teaspoon of filling in the centre. Draw up the edges and press together. Repeat to make 20 dumplings. Cover until ready to cook.

Arrange the dumplings in the steamer basket lined with parchment paper, making sure they do not touch each other (cook in batches, if necessary).

Steam over boiling water for 5 minutes.

Sprinkle with toasted sesame seeds and serve with a dipping sauce.

PORK & CABBAGE SHUMAI

Pork and cabbage are popular choices of dumpling fillings for home cooks in China because they are protein-packed yet inexpensive ingredients. But that doesn't stop these dumplings from being ridiculously tempting. Create the pretty flower shape by lightly squeezing the egg dough cup in the middle.

1 batch Egg Dough (see page 10)

FILLING

100 g/3½ oz. raw prawns/
   shrimp, peeled and deveined
100 g/3½ oz. lean minced/
   ground pork
60 g/1¼ cups chopped cabbage
1 tablespoon oyster sauce
½ tablespoon sesame oil
1 tablespoon cornflour/
   cornstarch
salt and ground white pepper
toasted sesame seeds,
   to garnish

DIPPING SAUCE

125 ml/½ cup soy sauce
2 tablespoons sesame oil
a large handful fresh coriander/
   cilantro, chopped
2 spring onions/scallions, sliced
1 teaspoon crushed/minced
   garlic
1 tablespoon grated fresh
   ginger

MAKES 16

For the filling, mince the prawns/shrimp by using a sharp knife to very finely chop into small pieces. Transfer to a large mixing bowl, add the rest of the filling ingredients, 1 teaspoon salt and 1 teaspoon ground white pepper, and mix thoroughly.

Use a sharp knife to slice the egg dough into 16 equal pieces. On a lightly floured surface, flatten each piece with a rolling pin until it has a round shape and a diameter of around 7.5 cm/3 in.

To assemble the shumai, place a wrapper on your palm and add a scant tablespoon of filling to the centre. Gather the edges of the wrapper and gently pleat so that a basket shape is formed up and around the filling, leaving the middle exposed. Lightly tap the base of the dumpling on the work surface to flatten the bottom and make sure there are no air pockets. Lightly squeeze the middle with your thumb and forefinger to create the classic flower shape. Repeat with the rest of the wrappers and filling.

Arrange the shumai at the bottom of the steamer basket lined with parchment paper, leaving plenty of space between each one (cook in batches, if necessary).

Steam the dumplings over boiling water for about 7 minutes, or until cooked through.

Make the dipping sauce while the dumplings are steaming by stirring the ingredients together in a small bowl.

Sprinkle with toasted sesame seeds and serve with the dipping sauce.

SALMON & MUSHROOM DUMPLINGS

Crystal skin dough is so pretty when cooked. The translucent effect shows off the colours of the delicate salmon and earthy mushrooms within.

1 batch Crystal Skin Dough
  (see page 10)

FILLING
1 oyster mushroom
1 bunch enoki mushrooms
3 shiitake mushrooms
20 g/¼ cup chanterelle
  mushrooms
1 tablespoon sunflower oil
1 garlic clove, finely chopped
1 small salmon fillet
1 tablespoon crushed/minced
  fresh ginger
1 Chinese chive,
  white parts removed
chilli/chili oil, to serve

a small round pastry/cookie cutter

MAKES 12

For the filling, slice the mushrooms into small, even pieces. Heat the sunflower oil in a frying pan/skillet and fry the mushrooms and garlic over a medium heat until fragrant. Set aside to cool, discarding any excess juice from the pan.

Roll out the crystal skin dough and stamp out 24 circles using the small round pastry/cookie cutter. Portion the salmon fillet into 12 pieces and cut the Chinese chive into 12 pieces, about 3 cm/1¼ in. in length.

Place a salmon piece in the centre of one dough circle, add a sprinkle of crushed/minced ginger and a chive piece neatly on the top. Lastly, top with a teaspoon of the cooked mushrooms. Cover with another round of crystal skin dough and press around the edge to seal.

Place the dumplings into the steamer basket lined with parchment paper, leaving space between them (cook in batches, if necessary).

Steam over boiling water for 15–20 minutes until transparent. Serve hot with chilli/chili oil.

PULLED PORK & OLIVE DUMPLINGS

Slow-cooked pork flavoured with five-spice and paired with the savoury tang of olives is a modern take on Asian dim sum that works so well.

1 batch Crystal Skin Dough
(see page 10)

FILLING
1 kg/2 lb. 4 oz. pork shoulder/
butt, bone in (once cooked
with bone and fat removed,
this should give roughly
250 g/9 oz. meat)
1 tablespoon dark muscovado
sugar
2 teaspoons Chinese five-spice
powder
35 g/⅓ cup pitted black olives,
chopped
salt

a roasting pan, lined with foil

MAKES 16

Preheat the oven to 220°C (425°F) Gas 7.

For the filling, place the pork shoulder/butt in the foil-lined roasting pan and pat the meat dry with paper towels. Mix the dark muscovado sugar and Chinese five-spice powder together with 1 tablespoon of salt and rub into the pork. Wrap the shoulder in the foil, making sure that it is fully enclosed.

Cook the pork in the preheated oven for 40 minutes, then turn the heat down to 125°C (250°F) Gas ½ and cook for a further 4–6 hours until the pork is very tender. (Check occasionally during cooking time that the pork is not drying out; add a little water if it is.)

Carefully unwrap the joint, strain and set aside the juices. Remove the bone and fat from the meat and discard. Use a fork to pull the pork into shreds. Mix the chopped olives into the pulled pork and set aside to cool.

Divide the crystal skin dough into 16 equal balls. On a lightly floured surface use a rolling pin to flatten the dough balls into thin discs, about 5 cm/2 in. in diameter. Cover the finished skins with a damp kitchen cloth as you work so that they don't dry out.

Place a large teaspoon of filling into the centre of a skin and gather the edges with your fingertips to make a round dumpling shape. Make small folds all the way around the top edge to create pleats. Pleat all the way around until the filling is enclosed. Repeat with the remaining skins and filling.

Place the dumplings in the steamer basket lined with parchment, leaving space between them (cook in batches, if necessary).

Steam over boiling water for 15–20 minutes, or until transparent. Warm the reserved pulled pork juices and place into dipping bowls. Serve the dumplings warm, with the warmed pork juices for dipping.

PEA SHOOT & PRAWN/SHRIMP DUMPLINGS

Pea shoots are leaf shoots of the mangetout, snowpea or garden pea. Sold in Chinese supermarkets and some greengrocers, they taste like essence of peas! Use mangetout/snowpeas if you can't find them.

1 batch Rice Flour Dough
   (see page 11)
extra fresh pea shoots or
   Chinese chives, to serve
dipping sauce of your choice,
   to serve

FILLING
250 g/5 small handfuls fresh
   pea shoots or mangetout/
   snowpeas, chopped
500 g/1 lb. 2 oz. raw prawns/
   shrimp, peeled, deveined and
   coarsely chopped (about
   250 g/9 oz. prepared weight)
4-cm/1½-in. piece fresh ginger,
   peeled and grated
1 tablespoon light soy sauce
1 tablespoon Shaoxing (Chinese
   rice wine) or dry sherry
   (optional)
1 teaspoon sesame oil
1 egg white, beaten

MAKES 32

Put the pea shoots or mangetout/snow peas in a colander and pour over boiling water, then quickly refresh under cold running water. Set aside.

Put the prawns/shrimp in a bowl and mix in the ginger, light soy sauce, Shaoxing or sherry, sesame oil and egg white. Set aside for 15 minutes to allow the flavours to develop. Add the chopped pea shoots or mangetout/snowpeas.

Line the steamer basket with banana leaves (or use parchment paper).

Divide the dough into 32 pieces, roll into balls and cover with a damp cloth. Dust a dry surface with flour and, using a rolling pin, roll out a ball of dough to a circle, 8 cm/3 in. in diameter. Put a heaped teaspoon of filling in the centre, brush the edges with water, then bring them together to enclose the filling. Twist to seal and break off any excess dough. Repeat with the remaining dough and filling, keeping the dumplings covered as you make them.

Put the dumplings, sealed-side down in the steamer basket, leaving space between them (cook in batches, if necessary).

Steam over boiling water for 7 minutes until the prawns/shrimp are cooked through. Serve warm with extra pea shoots or Chinese chives and a dipping sauce of your choice.

CHICKEN & POTATO CREAM STEW DUMPLINGS

These tasty morsels commemorate my love of canned chicken soup as a child. The mild and familiar flavours mean that these dumplings would be a great way of introducing young children to the idea of dim sum.

1 batch Crystal Skin Dough
   (see page 10)
melted butter, for dipping

FILLING
2 tablespoons unsalted butter
½ onion, finely chopped
½ carrot, finely diced
½ celery stalk, finely diced
1 potato, peeled and finely diced
1 tablespoon plain/all-purpose
   flour
1 chicken stock cube
175 ml/¾ cup milk
1 chicken breast, finely chopped
salt and freshly ground black
   pepper

MAKES 16

For the filling, melt the butter in a large pan over a medium heat. Add the onion, carrot, celery and potato. Cook, stirring occasionally, until tender, about 3–4 minutes.

Slowly whisk in the flour and cook for a minute, then crumble the stock cube into the pan and gradually add the milk, whisking constantly. Continue cooking and stirring until the sauce has thickened slightly, about 1–2 minutes.

Add the chicken. Bring the sauce to a boil, then reduce the heat and simmer until the potatoes and chicken are tender, about 12–15 minutes. Season with salt and pepper and set aside to cool.

Divide the crystal skin dough into 16 equal balls. On a lightly floured surface use a rolling pin to flatten the dough balls into thin discs, about 5 cm/2 in. in diameter. Cover the finished skins with a damp kitchen cloth as you work so that they don't dry out.

Place a large teaspoon of filling into the centre of each skin. Fold the dumplings in half and pinch the edges together to form a simple crescent shape.

Arrange the dumplings in the steamer basket lined with parchment, leaving space between them (cook in batches, if necessary).

Steam over boiling water for 15–20 minutes, or until the skins are transparent. Serve warm with hot melted butter for dipping.

SCALLOP & CRAB DUMPLINGS

The scallop is the pearlescent jewel in the crown of these dumplings, which are great for impressing guests at a dinner party. The spicy lime-based dipping sauce is the perfect complement to the luxurious seafood filling.

1 batch Crystal Skin Dough
   (see page 10)

FILLING
1 leek, finely chopped
60 g/2¼ oz. fresh crab meat
1 teaspoon crushed/minced
   fresh ginger
1 teaspoon crushed/minced
   garlic
½ teaspoon Shaoxing (Chinese
   rice wine) or dry sherry
½ teaspoon sugar
1 teaspoon vegetable or
   sunflower oil
1 teaspoon cornflour/cornstarch
16 scallops
salt and ground white pepper

DIPPING SAUCE
4 tablespoons sugar
2 tablespoons white vinegar
1 garlic clove, crushed/minced
1 tablespoon fish sauce
1 teaspoon Indonesian chilli/
   chili sauce
freshly squeezed juice of
   2 limes
a handful fresh coriander/
   cilantro, finely chopped

MAKES 16

Begin by making the dipping sauce. Place the sugar and vinegar in a small saucepan with 2 tablespoons water and bring to the boil. Boil until the sugar has dissolved, then turn down the heat to medium and stir in the garlic, fish sauce and chilli/chili sauce. Simmer for 1 minute, then remove from the heat. Allow to cool, then add the lime juice and coriander/cilantro. Set aside.

For the filling, in a bowl combine the leek, crab meat, ginger, garlic, Shaoxing or sherry, sugar, oil, cornflour/cornstarch and ½ teaspoon each salt and ground white pepper. Mix well.

Divide the crystal skin dough into 16 equal balls. On a lightly floured surface use a rolling pin to flatten the dough balls into thin discs, about 5 cm/2 in. in diameter. Cover the finished skins with a damp kitchen cloth as you work so that they don't dry out.

Put a large teaspoon of the crab mixture into the centre of each skin and place a scallop on the top. Fold the skin in half over the filling, and pinch together the sides to create the traditional crescent shaped dumpling. Fold the two ends of the dumpling inwards so that they overlap. Press together to seal and form the Chinese ingot shape.

Place the dumplings into the steamer basket lined with parchment paper, leaving space between them (cook in batches, if necessary).

Steam over boiling water for 15–20 minutes, or until the skins are transparent. Serve warm with the dipping sauce.

MEAT & POULTRY DISHES

STICKY RICE IN BANANA LEAVES WITH CHICKEN SKEWERS

Perfect for parties where you need a more substantial snack. Serve with a selection of sauces. You don't even need plates; the banana leaves (or foil) can do that job.

400 g/2¼ cups glutinous/sticky rice
750 ml/3 cups chicken stock
150 g/5¼ oz. banana leaves (or use foil)
2 red (bell) peppers, finely sliced
5-cm/2-in. piece fresh ginger, peeled and finely sliced
2 spring onions/scallions, sliced lengthways
a bunch of fresh coriander/cilantro, about 25 g/1 heaped cup
dipping sauces of your choice, to serve

CHICKEN SKEWERS
1 kg/2 lb. 4 oz. skinless, boneless chicken breast
125 ml/½ cup hoisin sauce
2 tablespoons chilli/chili sauce
2 tablespoons Shaoxing (Chinese rice wine) or dry sherry (optional)

12 bamboo skewers, soaked in water for 30 minutes

MAKES 12

To make the skewers, cut the chicken into 1.5-cm/½-in. cubes and thread onto the pre-soaked bamboo skewers. Mix the hoisin sauce in a shallow dish or tray with the chilli/chili sauce and Shaoxing or sherry, if using. Add the skewers, turn to coat, then cover and leave to marinate in the fridge for at least 2 hours.

Put the rice and chicken stock in a large saucepan and bring to the boil. Cover and simmer for 10 minutes, until part-cooked.

Wash the banana leaves and cut into 15-cm/6-in. squares. Divide the rice into 12 portions (about 4–5 tablespoons each) and put one portion in the middle of each banana leaf or foil square. Top with red (bell) pepper, ginger, spring onion/scallion and coriander/cilantro. Fold in the sides and secure with a cocktail stick/toothpick. Place in the steamer basket (cook in batches if needed).

Steam over boiling water for 10 minutes.

Meanwhile, heat a barbecue/outdoor grill or grill/broiler and cook the chicken for 6 minutes on each side.

Serve the rice parcels topped with the chicken skewers, with a selection of sauces on the side.

BOK CHOY ROLLS WITH SPICY CHICKEN

In Eastern Europe, meat and rice wrapped in cabbage is very popular. The idea lends itself very well to Chinese ingredients, making perfect dim sum. There are many popular vegetables from the cabbage family in Chinese cuisine – any, as long as the leaves are big enough, are suitable here.

100 g/½ cup plus 1 tablespoon long-grain rice

36 large Chinese leaves, such as large pak choi/bok choy, choi sum or Chinese cabbage, about 500 g/1 lb. 2 oz.

350 g/12 oz. skinless, boneless chicken breast, minced/ground

6 spring onions/scallions, chopped

2 garlic cloves, crushed/minced

4-cm/1½-in. piece fresh ginger, peeled and grated

2 green chillies/chiles, deseeded and finely chopped

2 teaspoons Chinese five-spice powder

2 tablespoons hoisin or yellow bean sauce

150 g/1 cup canned water chestnuts, drained and chopped

salt

plum sauce, to serve

MAKES 36

Boil the rice in salted water for 10 minutes, then drain.

Separate the leaves of the pak choi/bok choy, choi sum or cabbage – each should be at least 12.5 x 7.5 cm/5 x 3 in. Blanch in boiling water, then refresh in cold water. Set aside.

Put the chicken, spring onions/scallions, garlic, ginger, chillies/chiles, Chinese five-spice, hoisin or yellow bean sauce and water chestnuts in a bowl and mix well.

Put a tablespoon of the mixture in the centre of each leaf and roll up. Place in the steamer basket lined with parchment paper (cook in batches, if necessary).

Steam over boiling water for 10 minutes, then serve with plum sauce.

PEKING-STYLE DUCK PANCAKE WRAPS

Cooking traditional Peking duck is a time-consuming process involving drying, boiling and basting, not to mention the actual cooking! A much easier option is buying a ready prepared duck. Another simple solution is to use just the duck breast, which gives a succulent, simple result. These wraps always go down well at parties and are perfect picnic fare. The paper wrappers keep them moist and stop them sticking together if you prepare them in advance. Chinese Peking duck pancakes are sold by Chinese grocers – find them in the freezer or chiller cabinet.

4 duck breasts, 150 g/5¼ oz.
  each
4 tablespoons dark soy sauce
1 tablespoon clear honey
2 teaspoons Chinese five-spice
  powder
1 tablespoon groundnut/peanut
  oil
salt

TO SERVE
1 cucumber,
24 Chinese Peking duck
  pancakes
125 ml/½ cup hoisin sauce
6 spring onions/scallions,
  halved lengthways and
  crossways
sesame seeds

*24 squares of parchment paper,
  12-cm/5-in. square*

MAKES 24

Score the duck fat diagonally at 5-mm/¼-in. intervals and rub in about 1 tablespoon salt. Mix the soy sauce, honey and Chinese five-spice in a flat glass or ceramic dish. Put the duck breasts, skin-side up, in the marinade, moving them about so the flesh is coated. Cover and set aside in the fridge to marinate for at least 2 hours.

Remove the duck from the marinade and pat dry with paper towels.

Heat the oil in a frying pan/skillet over a medium heat, add the duck breasts, skin-side down, and cook for 8 minutes. Pour off the fat from the pan, then turn the breasts and cook the other side for 4 minutes. Remove from the pan and let cool.

Slice each duck breast diagonally into 12 strips.

Quarter the cucumber lengthways, then scoop out and discard the seeds. Slice each quarter in six lengthways and then in half crossways. You should have 48 pieces.

Place the pancakes in the steamer basket lined with parchment paper and steam over boiling water for 5 minutes.

When filling, work on 3–4 pancakes at a time and keep the others covered with a damp kitchen cloth so they don't dry out. Spread a teaspoon of hoisin sauce on each pancake, then add a couple of pieces of duck, a few strips of cucumber, a piece of spring onion/scallion and some sesame seeds. Fold up the bottom, then the sides. Wrap the pieces of parchment paper around the pancakes in the same way, then cover with a cloth until ready to serve.

CORIANDER/CILANTRO GINGER DUCK SALAD

You would need a super-size steamer to fit a whole duck. You can solve the space problem by cutting off the wings and keeping them for stock, and either steaming the legs separately or keeping them for another recipe.

a large bunch of fresh coriander/cilantro, plus extra to serve

7.5-cm/3-in. piece fresh ginger, peeled and sliced

3 garlic cloves, crushed/minced

1 duck, legs and wings removed

125 ml/½ cup mirin (Japanese rice wine)

100 ml/⅓ cup plus 1 tablespoon dark soy sauce

2 tablespoons sesame oil

2 tablespoons clear honey

grated zest of 1 lemon

2 bundles bean thread noodles (60 g/2 oz. total weight)

about 250 g/5 scant cups mixed salad leaves

a handful salted peanuts, toasted in a dry frying pan/ skillet

2–3 spring onions/scallions, sliced lengthways

SERVES 4

Wash the coriander/cilantro well, then put it into a bowl with the ginger and garlic. Mix well, then stuff into the duck cavity.

Put the duck onto a large, double sheet of foil, large enough to enclose it completely. Fold the foil along the top and scrunch the top closed. Fold and scrunch one end of the parcel closed.

Put a second double sheet of foil running the opposite way and scrunch closed at the sides, still keeping the end open. Put the duck, breast-side down, into a large steamer basket with the open end upwards.

Put the mirin, soy sauce, sesame oil, honey and lemon zest into a small saucepan and heat, stirring, to dissolve the honey. Pour half the mixture into the parcel and scrunch the foil closed, making sure no liquid runs out. Reserve the remainder.

Steam the duck over a large saucepan of boiling water for about 1½ hours, topping up with extra boiling water as necessary. Unwrap after 1 hour and test. The duck can be slightly rare. Once cooked to your liking, remove the duck from the steamer and let rest for about 10 minutes. Unwrap the foil and drain off and discard the liquid. Shred the meat from the duck and keep it warm.

Soak the noodles in hot water for 15 minutes, then drain and plunge into cold water. Drain, then toss in the reserved mirin mixture.

Arrange salad leaves on four plates, then add the cold noodles and shredded duck. Sprinkle with the toasted peanuts, spring onions/scallions and some extra coriander/cilantro. Spoon the remaining dressing from the noodles over the top and serve.

WONTON PORK MONEYBAGS

These can be cooked and served in bamboo steamers. If you cook three tiers at a time, you can serve the first batch while the next one is cooking. The bacon isn't a traditional Chinese ingredient, but it means you need less salt.

500 g/1 lb. 2 oz. minced/ground pork

125 g/1 cup raw prawns/shrimp, peeled and deveined

3 slices smoked streaky/fatty bacon, chopped

1 teaspoon crushed pepper, preferably Szechuan

1 egg white

2 teaspoons sesame oil

3-cm/1½-in. piece fresh ginger, peeled and grated

1 garlic clove, crushed/minced

2 teaspoons cornflour/cornstarch

4 spring onions/scallions

4 canned water chestnuts, finely diced

1 Chinese snake/yard-long bean or 4 green/French beans, thinly sliced

50 small fresh wonton wrappers (2 packs)

salt

banana leaves, for steaming (optional)

soy sauce, to serve

MAKES 50

Put the pork, prawns/shrimp and bacon into a food processor and blend to a purée. With the motor running, add the pepper, egg white, sesame oil, ginger, garlic, cornflour/cornstarch and 2 teaspoons salt.

Finely chop the white and green parts of the spring onions/scallions crossways, transfer to a mixing bowl, then add the pork mixture, water chestnuts and bean(s). Mix well – using your hands is the best way.

Cut the wonton wrappers into rounds and discard the trimmings – keep them covered with a damp kitchen cloth so they don't dry out. Line the steamer basket with banana leaves (or parchment paper).

Put a tablespoon of the pork filling in the centre of each round wrapper. Use a teaspoon to smooth the mixture almost to the edges.

Cup the wonton in the palm of your hand. Gather up your hand, pushing down with the teaspoon: you will achieve an open-topped, pleated, money-bag-shaped container filled with mixture. Drop it gently onto the work surface to flatten the bottom and settle the filling. Place in the steamer. Repeat until all are made, keeping the wrappers and the dumplings covered as you go and leaving space between the dumplings (cook in batches, if necessary).

Steam over boiling water for about 7–10 minutes, or until cooked through. Serve hot with a simple soy sauce dip.

QUAILS STUFFED WITH LIME & GINGER

In South-east Asia, small birds are stuffed with various flavourings, then steamed.
Quails are tiny, so serve two per diner; a poussin/spring chicken will serve one person
with other dishes alongside.

2 tablespoons groundnut/
   peanut oil
100 g/3½ oz. diced pancetta
1 shallot, chopped
4 garlic cloves, crushed/minced
2 tablespoons grated fresh
   ginger
dash of fish sauce (optional)
8 quails
8 tablespoons thick coconut
   cream
banana leaves, for steaming
   (optional)

SERVES 4

Heat the groundnut/peanut oil in a frying pan/skillet and add the pancetta, shallot, garlic and grated ginger. Stir-fry until crisp and golden – do not let the garlic burn. Taste and add fish sauce if needed.

Let cool a little, then use to stuff the quails.

Put each quail onto a piece of banana leaf (or use foil) and spoon a tablespoon of thick coconut cream over each one. Wrap up the parcels, scrunching up the foil or securing the leaves with a cocktail stick/ toothpick. Place in the steamer basket (cook in batches, if necessary).

Steam for 45 minutes–1 hour, or until cooked through. Open the parcels and serve.

VARIATION

Use the same technique to stuff poussins with lime and ginger. Soak 8 Chinese dried mushrooms in boiling water for 15 minutes. Slice 4 limes into wedges and use to stuff 4 poussins, along with a little sliced fresh ginger and a star anise in each poussin. Set aside. Pour 4 tablespoons honey into a bowl with 125 ml/½ cup mirin (Japanese rice wine), 4 tablespoons sesame oil, 4 tablespoons fish sauce and 4 star anise. Halve 8 spring onions/scallions lengthways and then crossways, and add to the bowl. Drain the soaked mushrooms, cut them into strips and add to the bowl. Stir well then divide between 4 bowls. Add a stuffed poussin to each and turn to coat well. Steam the birds, breast-side down, for 45 minutes, or until tender, turning them twice during cooking.

CURRIED RICE WITH STEAMED CHICKEN & FRESH PICKLE

This inspiration behind this one-pot dish originates in the Muslim south of Thailand. There all the ingredients – chicken, rice, herbs, spices and stock – are put in a large pot at the same time and cooked together. The flavours from the meat and other ingredients permeate the larger volume of rice, creating a delicious and flavourful dish. It makes an ideal one-pot meal to prepare at home.

3 tablespoons groundnut/ peanut or sunflower oil
4 large garlic cloves, finely chopped
500 g/2¾ cups fragrant Thai rice (jasmine rice), rinsed and drained
2 teaspoons curry powder
1 chicken, about 1.5 kg/3¼ lb., jointed
600 ml/2½ cups chicken stock
salt
fresh coriander/cilantro, to serve

FRESH PICKLE
5 tablespoons rice vinegar
3 teaspoons sugar
7.5-cm/3-in. piece cucumber
4 small shallots, finely chopped
2–3 small red chillies/chiles, thinly sliced
salt

a rice cooker (optional)

SERVES 4

Heat the oil in a wok or frying pan/skillet, add the garlic and fry until golden brown. Stir in the rice, then add the curry powder and 1 teaspoon salt. Add the chicken pieces and stir well.

To cook in a steamer, put the mixture in a heatproof bowl, add the stock and set in a steamer basket. Steam over boiling water for 30 minutes. Turn off the heat and set aside with the lid on for about 30 minutes for the chicken to finish cooking – check it is cooked through. Alternatively, transfer the mixture to an electric rice cooker, add the stock, cover and cook for 20 minutes, or until the chicken is cooked through.

While the chicken is steaming, make the pickle. Warm the vinegar, sugar and ½ teaspoon salt in a small saucepan, stirring until the sugar has dissolved. Remove from the heat. Cut the cucumber in half lengthways, scrape out the seeds with a teaspoon, then cut it in half again and slice very thinly. Add to the sauce with the chopped shallots and chillies/chiles. Stir well, pour into a small bowl and serve with the steamed chicken.

Slice the chicken and serve it with the curried rice, pickle and a handful of fresh coriander/cilantro.

SPICY DUCK WITH STICKY RICE

Laap is an original dish from Isaan, in the north-east of Thailand, where it will often be consumed with alcoholic drinks at social gatherings. In Thailand laap will often be made using beef, buffalo, river fish, prawns/shrimp, frogs and other wild animals. The dish is hot and spicy, usually with a mixture of hot chilli/chile, garlic and other ingredients that provide salty and sharp tastes. These bold flavours take centre stage in this laap-inspired dish made with duck breasts.

500 g/2¾ cups glutinous/sticky
   rice
1 tablespoon finely chopped
   lemongrass
1 tablespoon finely chopped
   galangal or ginger
3 tablespoons Thai fish sauce
3 tablespoons freshly squeezed
   lime juice (about 1½ limes)
2 teaspoons sugar
1 teaspoon chilli/chili powder
4 skinless duck breasts, finely
   chopped
5 small shallots, thinly sliced
4 spring onions/scallions, finely
   chopped
20 fresh mint leaves
raw crisp green vegetables,
   cut into bite-size pieces,
   to serve

SERVES 4

Put the rice in a bowl or pan, cover with water and let soak for at least 3 hours, or overnight if possible. Drain and rinse thoroughly.

Line the steamer basket with a double thickness of muslin/cheesecloth and spread the rice over the top. Steam over boiling water for 30 minutes.

Put the lemongrass, galangal, fish sauce, lime juice, sugar, chilli/chili powder and 2 tablespoons water in a saucepan and heat quickly. Add the duck and mix well until the meat is cooked through. Add the shallots and spring onions/scallions and cook for a few seconds more, then add the fresh mint leaves and remove from the heat.

Transfer to a serving dish and serve with a selection of raw crisp green vegetables and the steamed sticky rice.

STEAMED JAPANESE CUSTARD

Savoury custards are found all over East and South-east Asia. Ingredients can vary according to what's available, but, if you include meat or poultry, it should be cooked first.

1 chicken breast, brushed with soy sauce

about 20 small raw prawns/shrimp, peeled

1 thick trout fillet, cut into 2.5-cm/1-in. pieces

a handful dried black fungus, soaked in boiling water for 15 minutes, then drained

a large handful honigiri or enokitake mushrooms, roots trimmed

6 spring onions/scallions, the white and all the green, sliced diagonally

1 carrot, thinly sliced with a vegetable peeler, then sliced into strips

6 eggs

salad leaves, to garnish

DASHI MIXTURE

1 tablespoon shoyu (Japanese soy sauce)

1 tablespoon mirin (Japanese rice wine)

250 ml/1 cup dashi stock, made from instant dashi-bonito stock powder

SERVES 4

To make the dashi mixture, put the shoyu, mirin and made-up dashi stock into a saucepan and heat gently. Remove from the heat and plunge the pan into cold water to cool down the mixture as quickly as possible.

Meanwhile, put the chicken breast into the steamer basket and steam over boiling water for about 15 minutes, or until cooked through. Remove and pull into shreds.

Divide the chicken between four bowls. Divide the prawns/shrimp, trout, drained fungus (sliced into smaller pieces if necessary), honigiri or enokitake mushrooms, spring onions/scallions and carrot strips between the bowls, too.

Beat the eggs and strain them into a bowl, then stir in the cooled dashi mixture. Pour into the bowls, filling almost to the top, making sure some of the ingredients show through the surface. Cover with foil and put into the steamer basket.

Steam over boiling water for about 15 minutes. To test, remove the foil and press with your finger – the surface should be firm but yielding. If still liquid, steam for a few minutes longer until set.

Serve in the bowls with Chinese spoons and garnish with salad leaves.

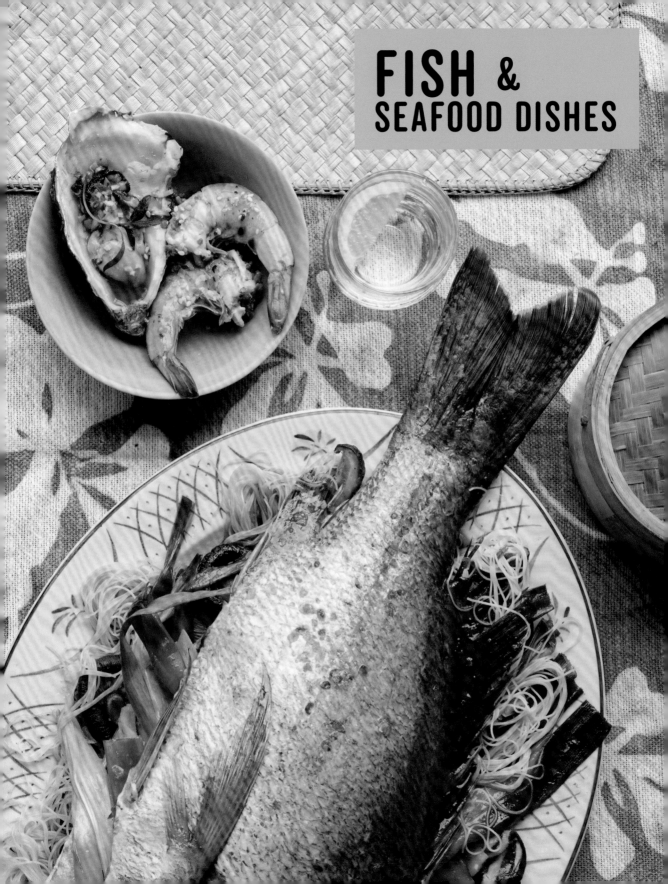

SALMON & ASIAN PESTO PARCELS

These delicate parcels with a hint of green herb and a pink cloud of salmon showing through translucent rice paper wrappers are a modern update on a Chinese classic. Serving with Asian pesto also gives them a new twist.

650 g/1 lb. 7 oz. skinless salmon
    fillet
20 rice paper wrappers
a small bunch of fresh
    coriander/cilantro, leaves only
1 tablespoon groundnut/peanut
    oil
dipping sauce of your choice,
    to serve

ASIAN PESTO
4 garlic cloves, crushed/minced
60 g/½ cup cashew nuts,
    chopped
a large bunch of coriander/
    cilantro, leaves only
a large bunch of Thai basil
    (or ordinary basil), leaves only
80 ml/⅓ cup groundnut/peanut
    oil

MAKES 20

To make the pesto, put all the ingredients in a small food processor and grind to a fairly smooth paste. Alternatively, use a mortar and pestle.

Cut the salmon into 20 even pieces, about 5-cm/2-in. square.

Dip a rice paper wrapper in warm water to soften, put a coriander/cilantro leaf in the centre, then top with a piece of salmon and a teaspoon of pesto. Fold in the sides to form a neat square (trim the edges if the wrapper is too big). The damp wrappers will stick closed. Repeat with the remaining wrappers and fillings.

Heat the oil in a frying pan/skillet and cook the parcels, in batches, sealed-side down, for 3 minutes until brown.

Transfer them to the steamer basket, leaving space between them. Steam over boiling water for 4–6 minutes until the salmon is cooked. Serve on their own or with a dipping sauce of your choice.

MUSSELS WITH EGG NOODLES & BLACK BEAN SAUCE

Chinese black beans, also known as salted black beans or fermented black beans, are sold packed in plastic bags in larger supermarkets and Chinese food stores. Although you could use ready-made black bean sauce, it's worth making your own, as it is very simple and makes a world of difference to the flavour.

125 g/1¼ cups fresh or dried egg noodles
1 tablespoon sesame oil
24 green-lipped mussels, cooked
a small bunch of fresh coriander/cilantro

BLACK BEAN SAUCE
1 tablespoon groundnut/peanut oil
2 garlic cloves, crushed/minced
5-cm/2-in. piece fresh ginger, peeled and finely shredded
4 spring onions/scallions, thinly sliced
2 teaspoons cornflour/cornstarch
2 tablespoons Chinese black beans, lightly crushed

MAKES 24

Cook the noodles in boiling water until just done, about 3–4 minutes for fresh or 7–9 minutes for dried. Drain and then toss in a bowl with the sesame oil.

To make the black bean sauce, heat the groundnut/peanut oil in a small wok or saucepan, add the garlic, ginger and spring onions/scallions and cook for 2 minutes. Put the cornflour/cornstarch in a small bowl with 1 tablespoon water, stir until smooth, then add enough water to make 100 ml/⅓ cup plus 1 tablespoon. Add the black beans and cornflour/cornstarch mixture to the wok. Bring to the boil and stir until thickened, about 2 minutes. Toss with the noodles.

Discard one of each pair of mussel shells, so each mussel sits in its half shell. Loosen the mussel if necessary. Place the mussels in the steamer basket. Twist a fork into the noodles, taking a small amount to arrange in each mussel shell.

Steam the mussels and noodles over boiling water for 5 minutes. Scatter with chopped coriander/cilantro and serve immediately.

JAPANESE-STYLE OYSTERS WITH MIRIN & GINGER

Oysters can be big or little, according to where you live, but large, assertively flavoured oysters are the best for cooking. Use 3–5 per person, depending on size. You can change the emphasis of this dish with different flavourings: try lime zest, lemongrass and ginger for a South-east Asian taste.

12–20 oysters, depending
    on size
4 spring onions/scallions
1 tablespoon Japanese pickled
    ginger, thinly sliced

MIRIN & GINGER SAUCE
125 ml/½ cup mirin
    (Japanese rice wine)
3 tablespoons white rice vinegar
3 tablespoons shoyu (Japanese
    soy sauce) or fish sauce (for
    a South-east Asian flavour)
2.5-cm/1-in. piece fresh ginger,
    peeled and finely chopped
4 spring onions/scallions,
    thinly sliced

SERVES 4

Open the oysters, or get the fishmonger to do it for you. If the latter, make sure this is done a very short time before you cook them.

Trim the spring onions/scallions, halve them crossways into white and green, then thinly slice lengthways.

For the sauce, put the mirin, vinegar, shoyu, ginger and spring onions/scallions into a small saucepan and stir over a low heat until just warm.

Put the oysters onto a plate in the steamer basket (if the oysters are large, you may have to use several layers). Spoon 1 teaspoon of the dressing into each one.

Steam over boiling water for about 2 minutes, then serve sprinkled with the spring onions/scallions and pickled ginger.

NOTE Remember, you aren't cooking the oysters, merely heating them. If you cook them, they'll shrink – just heat them, and you'll develop their flavours.

SPICY HOT MUSSELS

These mussels glory under the name of hoy mang poo, which is such a great name, that a version of the dish had to be included here. Mussels and clams are perfectly designed for eating with chopsticks.

2 kg/4 lb. 7 oz. (approx. 80–90) mussels (or clams, or a mixture of both)

5-cm/2-in. piece fresh ginger or galangal, peeled and chopped

2 stalks lemongrass, trimmed, peeled, and thinly sliced

a handful fresh coriander/cilantro, leaves only, plus the roots if available, chopped

2 makrut lime leaves, very finely shredded crossways, or the grated zest of 1 lime

a handful Thai basil leaves, torn (optional)

2–4 red bird's eye chillies/chiles

3 garlic cloves, crushed/minced

5 Thai pink shallots or 1 regular, sliced

250 ml/1 cup fish stock

3 tablespoons fish sauce

freshly squeezed juice of 1 lime

CHILLI DIPPING SAUCE

freshly squeezed juice of 1 lime

3 tablespoons fish sauce

1–2 red bird's eye chillies/chiles, crushed

2 garlic cloves, crushed/minced

2 teaspoons sugar

SERVES 4

Check the mussels by tapping each one against a work surface. They should close tightly – discard any that remain open. Scrub the shells with a small brush and remove the wiry beards. Rinse and arrange in a bowl in the steamer basket – the bowl should be deep enough to catch all the juices the mussels produce.

Put the ginger, lemongrass, coriander/cilantro, lime leaves and basil, if using, into a small food processor and work to a paste. Add the chillies/chiles, garlic and shallots and blend again. Alternatively, use a mortar and pestle. Stir in the stock, fish sauce and lime juice, then pour over the mussels.

Steam over boiling water until the mussels open, discarding any that fail to open.

To make the dipping sauce, put the lime juice, fish sauce, chillies/chiles, garlic and sugar into a bowl. Mix well, then divide between four small dipping bowls and serve with the mussels.

PRAWNS/SHRIMP STUFFED WITH CHILLI/CHILI JAM

*South-east Asian chilli/chili pastes are some of the world's favourite spicy mixtures —
complex and delicious. You'll need lots of hot towels to mop up spicy fingers after eating
this hands-on dish. Serve 3–5 prawns/shrimp per person.*

12–20 large raw prawns/shrimp,
    depending on size
4 tablespoons mirin
    (Japanese rice wine)
freshly squeezed juice of 1 lime,
    plus 3 extra limes, halved,
    to serve

CHILLI/CHILI JAM
125 g/1¾ cups dried shrimp
8 garlic cloves, unpeeled
10 Thai pink shallots,
    or 2 regular
2 tablespoons groundnut/
    peanut oil
12 large dried red chillies/chiles,
    medium hot, broken in half
    and deseeded
1 tablespoon tamarind paste
2 tablespoons brown sugar
1 tablespoon fish sauce

SERVES 4

Preheat the oven to 200°C (400°F) Gas 6.

To make the chilli/chili jam, put the dried shrimp onto a piece of foil
and crumple up the edges. Put onto a baking sheet. Add the garlic
and shallots to the baking sheet and cook in the preheated oven for
10 minutes. Remove the shrimp and return the baking sheet to the
oven for a further 20 minutes until dark brown and aromatic.

Put 1 tablespoon of the oil into a small frying pan/skillet, add the chillies/
chiles and stir-fry for a few seconds to release the aromas. Grind to a meal
with a mortar and pestle or in a blender, then add the shrimp and grind
again. Add the garlic and shallots and grind again.

Put the tamarind paste into a small bowl and stir in 2 tablespoons water,
the sugar and fish sauce.

Add the remaining 1 tablespoon oil to the frying pan/skillet, add the chilli/
chile mixture and heat until aromatic. Stir in the tamarind mixture and
cook until thick. Set aside until cool enough to handle. Store any leftover
mixture in the fridge for up to 3 days.

Cut down the backs of the unshelled prawns/shrimp and remove the vein.
Press some chilli/chili jam into the back cut, pushing it between the shell
and flesh as much as possible. Put onto a plate in the steamer basket and
sprinkle with the mirin and lime juice.

Steam over boiling water until just opaque. Do not overcook or the
prawns/shrimp will be tough. Serve with lime halves, extra chilli/chili
jam and hot towels.

BLUE SWIMMER CRABS WITH CHILLI/CHILE, LIME & GINGER

Crabs are becoming somewhat expensive these days – and smaller. There is a particular variety, the pretty Blue Swimmer, which is lovely for this dish. Use whatever crabs are popular where you live. Steaming is a delicious way to prepare crabs – they don't become watery, as they sometimes do when boiled.

4–8 swimmer crabs, depending
on size, or 2 larger crabs
6 spring onions/scallions, sliced

LIME & GINGER DRESSING
4 tablespoons groundnut/
peanut oil
4 tablespoons mirin
(Japanese rice wine)
5-cm/2-in. piece fresh ginger,
peeled and thinly sliced
freshly squeezed juice of
2 limes
2 teaspoons sugar
2 tablespoons fish sauce
2 red chillies/chiles, thinly sliced

SERVES 4

To make the dressing, heat the oil in a wok or small saucepan, add the mirin, ginger, lime juice (reserve the squeezed lime halves), sugar, fish sauce and chillies/chiles and stir-fry for about 1 minute. Add 1 tablespoon water and the squeezed lime halves, and cook for a further 1 minute. Remove from the heat and set aside.

Put the crabs into the steamer basket. Steam over boiling water until they have turned red.

Remove from the steamer, let cool a little, then prise off the shells and remove the feathery sections from the bodies. Break or cut the bodies into two, four or eight pieces, depending on size, then put the bodies and top shells into the wok.

Stir-fry briskly to coat with the sauce, then toss the sliced spring onions/scallions over the top.

Transfer to a serving platter and serve with crab picks or chopsticks to push out the flesh, plus hot towels for wiping your hands later.

MALAYSIAN FISH PARCELS

Banana leaves are the traditional wraps for this Malaysian-inspired dish, but you could also use foil or even greaseproof paper. Use a firm fish – though Malaysia doesn't have salmon, it is widely available and marries well with spicy flavours. Be warned – this one's hot! If you want something slightly less fiery, use fewer chillies/chiles.

600 g/1 lb. 5 oz. firm boneless
   fish, such as salmon,
   mackerel or cod
4 eggs
3 makrut lime leaves, central
   stems removed and
   remainder thinly sliced
250 ml/1 cup coconut cream
banana leaves, for wrapping
   (optional)
salt

CHILLI/CHILE PASTE
5 dried chillies/chiles, soaked in
   boiling water for 15 minutes
5 red bird's eye chillies/chiles,
   chopped
5 Thai pink shallots or 1 regular
2 garlic cloves, crushed/minced
2 stalks lemongrass, trimmed,
   peeled and thinly sliced
2.5-cm/1-in. piece fresh ginger,
   peeled and sliced
1 tablespoon fish sauce
1 teaspoon ground turmeric

MAKES 2

Cut the fish into pieces 5 x 2.5 cm/2 x 1 in., sprinkle with 1 teaspoon salt and set aside for 15 minutes.

To make the chilli/chile paste, drain the soaked chillies/chiles and put into a small blender. Add the bird's eye chillies/chiles, shallots, garlic, lemongrass, ginger, fish sauce and turmeric and blend well. Alternatively, use a mortar and pestle.

Put the eggs into a bowl and beat lightly with a fork. Add the chilli/chile paste and lime leaves and stir well. Stir in the coconut cream and 1 teaspoon salt.

Wash and dry the banana leaves, if using (you can use foil instead). Warm them over an open flame for a few seconds until softened, then cut into pieces about 17.5 x 15 cm/7 x 6 in.

Put a piece of fish in the centre of each piece of leaf. Bring the two long sides together, then fold one of the short sides so the middle meets the two long edges. Fold the wings back and keep together (you could use a paperclip or plastic clothes peg/clothes pin). Add about 2 tablespoons of the egg mixture to the parcel and fold the other end in the same way. Fasten with a long cocktail stick/toothpick or bamboo skewer. You can also trim the top with scissors to make a neat parcel, if you like. Place in the steamer basket.

Steam over boiling water for 20 minutes, then serve with a selection of other Asian dishes.

STEAMED STUFFED BABY SQUID

Some of the ingredients for this stuffing – lemongrass, chilli/chile paste, lime leaves, makrut limes and grated ginger – can be frozen and used from frozen. The squid usually have their pink skin rubbed off: try leaving it on – it looks pretty and tastes wonderful.

500 g/1 lb. 2 oz. baby squid, about 5–7.5 cm/2–2½ in. long, thawed if frozen
dipping sauce of your choice, to serve

STUFFING
3 makrut lime leaves
3 stalks lemongrass
1 makrut lime, preferably frozen
2 teaspoons green Thai curry paste
1 shallot, chopped
1 garlic clove, crushed/minced
3-cm/1½-in. piece fresh ginger, peeled and grated
2 tablespoons mirin (Japanese rice wine)
2 tablespoons fish sauce
1 bundle beanthread noodles (about 30 g/1 oz.)
2 Italian cured coarse pork sausages
2 tablespoons groundnut/ peanut or sunflower oil

SERVES 4

To clean the squid, pull the tentacles out of the bodies, cut off and chop the tentacles and reserve them. Remove and discard the transparent quill and rinse out the bodies.

To make the stuffing, cut the central vein out of the makrut lime leaves and very finely chop the remainder. Remove the outer leaves of the lemongrass, thinly slice the lower 5 cm/2 in. of each stalk and discard the rest.

Finely grate the makrut lime zest. Cut off and discard the white pith, then grate half the lime, either refreezing or discarding the remainder. Put the curry paste, shallot, garlic and ginger into a bowl, then stir in the lime zest and grated lime, lime leaves, lemongrass, mirin and fish sauce.

Put the noodles into a second bowl and cover with hot water. Set aside for 15 minutes, then drain and cover with cold water. Just before using, drain again and chop into short sections with scissors.

Scrape the pork meat out of the sausages, discarding the skins. Add the meat to the bowl of stuffing. Using a hand-held stick blender, work to a paste. Heat the oil in a frying pan/skillet or wok and stir-fry the mixture until the pork is cooked and dried out, about 5 minutes. Transfer to a bowl and put the bowl into a pan of cold water to cool quickly. When cool, stir in the noodles and chopped tentacles.

Fill each squid body with the pork and noodle mixture. Use your fingers, or a bottle-filling funnel and a chopstick as a pusher. As each body is filled, secure it with a cocktail stick/toothpick. If serving as finger food, put another stick through the other end, too.

Arrange in a single layer in the steamer basket, leaving space between them (cook in batches if necessary).

Steam for 10 minutes, then serve with a dipping sauce of your choice. If using as finger food, cut in half before serving.

CHINESE STEAMED FISH

Chinese cooks are very discerning in choosing their fish – they like a fine textured fish with good flavour for this dish. Here grouper is used, but moonfish, parrotfish or red snapper are also good. Take the lid of the steamer with you when you buy the fish to ensure it will fit.

4–5 Chinese dried mushrooms, soaked in boiling water for 15 minutes
1 bundle beanthread noodles (about 30 g/1 oz.)
1 large whole fish, such as grouper or snapper (about 1 kg/2 lb. 4 oz., cleaned and scaled)
5-cm/2-in. piece fresh ginger, peeled and very thinly sliced
3 garlic cloves, crushed/minced
6 spring onions/scallions, thinly sliced lengthways
1 tablespoon groundnut/peanut oil
2 tablespoons soy sauce or fish sauce
1 teaspoon sugar
2 tablespoons Shaoxing (Chinese rice wine) or dry sherry
salt

SERVES 4

Drain the mushrooms, remove the stems if any, then slice the caps.

Put an oval serving plate into a large steamer. Put the dried noodles onto the plate, then add the sliced mushrooms.

Rinse the fish in salted water, then pat dry with paper towels. Stuff the cavity with the ginger, garlic and half the spring onions/scallions, then brush the skin with the oil. Blanch the remaining spring onions/scallions in boiling water for 10 seconds, then drain.

Put the fish onto the plate on top of the noodles and mushrooms. Mix the soy sauce, sugar and Shaoxing in a bowl, then sprinkle over the fish.

Steam over boiling water until the flesh is opaque, about 20–30 minutes depending on the thickness of the fish. Add more boiling water if needed.

Remove the plate and wipe the underside dry. Discard the flavourings from the cavity, but leave the noodles and mushrooms, which soak up lots of flavour. Add the blanched spring onions/scallions and serve.

SPICY SALMON POTS

Steamed in small ceramic bowls, this spicy salmon dish is inspired by banana leaf cups. Instead of the banana leaf, strips of pandanus are used – a delicious ingredient that adds scent and a pretty green colour to some South-east Asian dishes. Omit if unavailable.

1 egg, beaten
350 ml/1½ cups thick coconut cream
1 tablespoon rice flour
500 g/1 lb. 2 oz. salmon fillet, sliced crossways into fine strips
1–3 red bird's eye chillies/chiles, deseeded and thinly sliced, plus extra to serve
2 tablespoons Thai green curry paste
1½ tablespoons fish sauce
2 spring onions/scallions, thinly sliced
4 pandanus leaves (optional, see note)
4 makrut lime leaves, bruised with a fork
micro herbs, to garnish (optional)

4 small bowls or ramekins, greased with groundnut/peanut oil

SERVES 4

Put the egg into a mixing bowl, add the coconut cream and rice flour and whisk well. Reserve 4 tablespoons of the mixture. Add the strips of fish to the mixing bowl, then stir in the chillies/chiles, curry paste, fish sauce and spring onions/scallions.

Line the greased small bowls or ramekins with strips of pandanus leaf, if using.

Divide half the fish mixture between the small bowls or ramekins and put into the steamer basket. Wrap the lid of the steamer in a cloth to stop the condensation dropping back into the bowls.

Steam over boiling water for 7 minutes, then divide the remaining fish mixture between the bowls. Add a lime leaf to each, then pour over the reserved 4 tablespoons of the coconut cream mixture.

Steam until firm, then serve, topped with a few slices of chilli/chile and garnish with micro herbs.

NOTE Pandanus, kewra or screwpine leaves are found in Asian markets. Indian stores sometimes have kewra water – add just a drop to the coconut cream mixture to appreciate the scent.

JAPANESE STEAMED FISH ON NOODLES WITH SEAWEED

This is a very elegant and stylish dish, and easy to make – the bowls can be assembled beforehand, then cooked at the very last minute. The traditional Japanese practice of salting the fish increases the succulence of its flesh when cooked – a great secret for all fish cooks!

1 salmon fillet (about 500–750 g/
   1 lb. 2 oz.–1 lb. 10 oz.)
1 bundle soba buckwheat
   noodles (about 125 g/4 oz.)
1 bundle green tea noodles
   (cha-somen, about 125 g/4 oz.)
1 sheet kombu seaweed, wiped
   with a cloth, then cut into
   4 pieces (optional, see note)
4 tablespoons sake
salt

DASHI SAUCE
250 ml/1 cup dashi stock
175 ml/¾ cup mirin
   (Japanese rice wine)
175 ml/¾ cup shoyu
   (Japanese soy sauce)
a handful dried bonito flakes
   (optional)

SERVES 4

Cut the salmon crossways into four strips and put the pieces, skin-side down, onto a plate sprinkled with a layer of salt. Set aside for 20 minutes, then rinse off the salt and pat dry with paper towels.

Bring a large saucepan of water to the boil, add the noodles and cook, stirring a little with chopsticks, until the water returns to the boil. Add a splash of cold water and return to the boil. Repeat this twice more until the noodles are *al dente* – a total of 3–4 minutes. Drain, rinse in cold water and set aside.

When ready to assemble, dip the noodles into boiling water and drain. Put pieces of kombu seaweed, if using, into four lidded ceramic bowls (alternatively, use bowls with a small saucer as a lid). Add a pile of noodles and top with a fish fillet, skin-side up.

Sprinkle 1 tablespoon sake over each one, put a circle of foil on top and the lid on top of that. Put the bowls into the steamer basket.

Steam over boiling water for about 10 minutes, or until the fish is cooked, but still pink in the middle.

Put the dashi sauce ingredients into a saucepan, bring to the boil and, when ready to serve, strain over the fish. Serve with chopsticks and small spoons. Heavenly!

NOTE The kombu seaweed is there for flavour – discard before eating.

STEAMED TOFU/BEANCURD SKIN WITH WILD MUSHROOM FILLING

Tofu/beancurd skins soak up the rich flavours of the mushrooms and gochujang (Korean red pepper paste) as they soften in the steamer. Dried tofu/beancurd skins will need to be soaked according to the packet instructions before use.

100 g/3½ oz. wood ear/cloud ear mushrooms, soaked in water for 24 hours

150 g/5¼ oz. shiitake mushrooms

150 g/5¼ oz. king oyster mushrooms

200 g/7 oz. enoki mushrooms

2 carrots

1 yellow (bell) pepper

100 g/3½ oz. Chinese chives

3 tablespoons vegetable or sunflower oil

1 tablespoon chopped garlic

2 teaspoons ground ginger

1 tablespoon Korean gochujang (red pepper paste)

2 tablespoons light soy sauce

8 sheets soft tofu/beancurd skin, 10-cm/4-in. square

salt and freshly ground black pepper

MAKES 8

Drain the wood ear/cloud ear mushrooms, then slice them thinly along with all the other mushrooms.

Julienne the carrots, (bell) pepper and Chinese chives into thin strips about 6 cm/2½ in. long.

Heat the oil in a frying pan/skillet, add the mushrooms and fry until they are softened. Add the garlic and ginger and continue to fry until fragrant. Add the julienned vegetables and give the pan a quick toss, then add the gochujang, soy sauce and 250 ml/1 cup water. Bring it to a simmer and cook for a few minutes, then season with salt and pepper to taste and remove from the heat. Allow the mixture to cool.

Strain the filling through a fine-mesh sieve/strainer, reserving the strained sauce, then divide the filling into eight portions.

Arrange the tofu/beancurd skins on the work surface and add a portion of filling to each, placing it at the base of the sheet. Roll each sheet around the filling, then place the filled rolls in a heatproof dish.

Pour over the reserved sauce and place the dish into the steamer basket.

Steam over boiling water for 10 minutes until the tofu/beancurd skin has softened. Allow to cool a little before serving with the sauce from the base of the dish.

STEAMED EGGS WITH SILKEN TOFU/BEANCURD

This savoury steamed egg dish is lovely served alongside a variety of other Asian dishes. It has a beautifully smooth texture – be careful not to steam it over too high a heat, as this can curdle the mixture and spoil its smooth finish.

2 salted duck eggs

4 eggs

1 tablespoon fried shallots

300-g/10½-oz. packet Japanese
   silken tofu/beancurd

1 tablespoon sesame oil

1 tablespoon soy sauce

salt and freshly ground black
   pepper

spring onions/scallions,
   thinly sliced, to garnish

thinly sliced seaweed,
   to garnish

SERVES 4

Separate the salted eggs and put the salted egg yolks onto a chopping board. Cut the salted egg yolks into quarters. Set aside. The whites are not used in this recipe.

Crack the hen's eggs into a bowl and whisk with 500 ml/2 cups water. Add the cut up egg yolks, fried shallots and 1 teaspoon each of salt and pepper. Give it a stir.

Place the whole piece of tofu/beancurd into a round heatproof dish and pour the egg mixture around it. Place into the steamer basket.

Steam over boiling water for 10–20 minutes until set. Do not steam over very high heat or it will curdle and not be smooth.

Add the sesame oil and soy sauce to finish, and garnish with thinly sliced spring onions/scallions and seaweed to serve.

STUFFED FRESH TOFU/BEANCURD WITH BROCCOLI & VEGETABLE SAUCE

This dish uses the whole broccoli head. The vibrant green florets are stuffed into the tofu/beancurd pockets, while the stalk is whizzed up in a blender or food processor to make a paste for the sauce. Nutritious and delicious.

600 g/1 lb. 5 oz. fresh medium tofu/beancurd
1 head broccoli
1 tablespoon sunflower or vegetable oil
1 brown onion, thinly sliced
2 garlic cloves, chopped
1 tablespoon grated fresh ginger
2 red chillies/chiles, deseeded and thinly sliced
30 g/1 oz. goji berries, soaked in water for 1 hour
60 g/2 oz. pickled mustard stems, chopped
2 teaspoons ground Szechuan pepper
2 teaspoons potato starch

MAKES 6

Cut the tofu into six 100-g/3½-oz. square chunks. Place them in a round heatproof dish.

Use a sharp fruit knife to slice a pocket into each chunk of tofu/beancurd without cutting all the way through.

Break the broccoli into florets, reserving the stalk. Slice the broccoli florets and stuff them into the tofu pockets.

Peel the broccoli skin off the stalk, then place the peeled raw stalk in a food processor or blender and blitz it into a paste.

Heat the oil in a wok over a medium heat and lightly fry the onion, garlic and ginger until fragrant but not browned. Add the chillies/chiles, broccoli paste, drained goji berries, mustard stems and Szechuan pepper and cook for 1 minute.

Mix the potato starch into 375 ml/1½ cups water, then add to the wok to make a sauce (add more water if the sauce is too thick).

Pour the sauce over the broccoli-stuffed tofu/beancurd and place the dish into the steamer basket.

Steam over boiling water for 6–8 minutes, removing when the broccoli turns dark green. Serve.

GREEN VEGETABLES WITH LEMON SOY BUTTER

Green vegetables, such as peas and beans, love steam and stay deliciously crunchy. Use any combination, according to what's available that day. Butter isn't a traditional ingredient in East and South-east Asia, but is now seen more and more. With lemon and soy, it makes a delicious dressing – for Western dishes, too.

8 baby courgettes/zucchini or pattypans, green or yellow, halved lengthways

4 Chinese snake/yard-long beans, cut into 10-cm/4-in. lengths (optional)

100 g/3½ oz. fine green/French beans, stalk ends trimmed

125 g/1 cup peas, fresh or frozen

12 small asparagus tips

100 g/1 heaped cup sugar snap peas

100 g/1 heaped cup mangetout/snow peas, halved lengthways (optional)

LEMON SOY BUTTER

125 g/9 tablespoons unsalted butter

6 spring onions/scallions, sliced crossways

3-cm/1½-in. piece fresh ginger, peeled and grated

1 teaspoon Japanese seven-spice (shichimi togarishi) or freshly ground black pepper

125 ml/½ cup sake

freshly squeezed juice of 1–1½ lemons (about 125 ml/½ cup)

2 tablespoons shoyu (Japanese soy sauce)

SERVES 4

To make the lemon soy butter, put the butter into a saucepan, add the spring onions/scallions, ginger, seven-spice, sake, lemon juice and shoyu, and heat gently. Set aside, but keep the mixture warm.

Prepare a bowl of iced water.

Add the courgettes/zucchini to the steamer basket and steam over boiling water for about 1 minute. Transfer to the iced water to stop the cooking.

Add both kinds of beans and the asparagus to the steamer basket and steam over boiling water until all are tender but crisp. Transfer to the iced water to stop the cooking.

Put the peas into a small, heatproof bowl and add to the steamer basket. Add the sugar snaps and mangetout/snow peas and steam over boiling water until just tender – as each is done, transfer to the iced water.

When all are done, drain in a colander, then put the colander into the steamer to reheat the vegetables, about 2 minutes.

Transfer to a warm serving dish, pour over the lemon soy butter and serve as an accompaniment to other dishes.

CHINESE GREENS WITH STAR ANISE BUTTER

Steaming is the perfect way to cook most leafy greens. They keep their nutrients and bright colour and need just a sprinkle of sauce to give them spark. Simple oyster or mushroom sauces are great on greens, but butter flavoured with whole star anise is something special.

500 g/1 lb. 2 oz. Asian greens, such as Chinese broccoli, Chinese flowering cabbage or mustard cabbage, choi sum or baby pak choi/bok choy, purple sprouting broccoli or broccoli florets, or regular cabbage, thickly sliced

STAR ANISE BUTTER
3 whole star anise
125 g/9 tablespoons unsalted butter
½ teaspoon soy sauce, or to taste
1 tablespoon sesame oil
6 spring onions/scallions, trimmed and sliced crossways

SERVES 4

To make the star anise butter, put the star anise into small saucepan, add the butter, soy sauce, sesame oil and spring onions/scallions and melt over a low heat. Set aside to infuse while you cook the greens.

Place the chosen greens in the steamer basket and steam over boiling water until just tender. Choi sum and pak choi/bok choy will take about 4 minutes, or until the leaves are just wilted and the stems tender (take care not to overcook). Broccoli will take a few minutes longer.

To serve, transfer the greens to a plate, reheat the dressing, pour over the greens and serve.

NOTE If you're using any member of the cabbage family, don't cook it for more than about 7 minutes. After that time, it develops that infamous cabbagey smell. In any case, it will taste much nicer if it's still crunchy.

TWO-RICE PEARL BALLS

This dim sum goes under many names, including 'lion's head', 'porcupine' and 'pearl' – all because of the grains of rice sticking to the outside of the meatball. This recipe calls for black and white glutinous/sticky rice, but if black is unavailable, just white is fine.

100 g/½ cup plus 1 tablespoon
    white glutinous/sticky rice
100 g/½ cup plus 1 tablespoon
    black glutinous/sticky rice
300 g/1½ scant cups minced/
    ground beef
150 g/5 cups shiitake
    mushrooms, finely chopped
6 shallots or 1 small onion,
    finely chopped
2 garlic cloves, crushed/minced
4-cm/1½-in. piece fresh ginger,
    peeled and grated
1 egg, beaten
4 tablespoons mushroom soy
    sauce or oyster sauce
salt
dipping sauce of your choice,
    to serve (optional)

MAKES 32

Put the white and black rice in two separate saucepans, add 125 ml/1 cup water and 1 teaspoon salt to each and bring to the boil. Drain immediately and rinse well.

Put the beef in a bowl, add the mushrooms, shallots or onion, garlic, ginger, beaten egg and soy or oyster sauce and mix well.

Make 32 balls of mixture, about 1 teaspoon each, rolling with wet hands. Mix the black and white rice together, then roll the meatballs in the rice so they are well coated.

Line the steamer basket with parchment paper and arrange the pearl balls about 2.5 cm/1 in. apart.

Steam over boiling water for 30 minutes until the rice is cooked.

Serve alone or with a dipping sauce of your choice.

STEAMED JAPANESE VEGETARIAN RICE

This simple vegetarian dish uses Japanese short-grain rice and five-grain rice (a mix of grains, available from Asian supermarkets) to create a varied texture between the grains. Serve it as a side dish or as part of a larger spread of vegetarian Asian dishes.

45 g/¼ cup five-grain rice, soaked in water for 2 hours

380 g/2 cups Japanese short-grain rice

80 g/2¾ oz. raw whole chestnuts, peeled

60 g/2 oz. edamame beans

20 g/¾ oz. goji berries, soaked in water for 1 hour

salt

1 spring onion/scallion, shredded, to serve

SERVES 6

Drain the five-grain rice and wash it, along with the Japanese short-grain rice, under running water until the water is clear and all the excess starch has gone. Place both types of rice into a heatproof dish and add 625 ml/ 2½ cups water. Leave to soak for 15 minutes.

Add the peeled chestnuts, edamame beans, drained goji berries and 1 teaspoon salt. Give it a stir, then place in the steamer basket and steam over boiling water for 30 minutes.

Let it rest for 10 minutes off the heat before carefully removing the rice from the steamer basket.

Serve topped with shredded spring onion/scallion.

BABY (BELL) PEPPERS WITH SPICY PEANUTS

Made with tiny (bell) peppers, about 5-cm/2-in. long, these make excellent two-bite-size finger food for parties. If you can't find baby (bell) peppers, use larger ones and cut them in half crossways. You could also use very mild, largish chilli/chile peppers.

500 g/1 lb. 2 oz. baby sweet (bell) peppers

PEANUT FILLING
1 bundle beanthread vermicelli noodles (about 30 g/1 oz.)
100 g/¾ cup roasted salted peanuts
1 tablespoon red Thai curry paste
1 garlic clove, crushed/minced
grated zest and freshly squeezed juice of 1 lime
1 tablespoon sugar
1 tablespoon sesame oil

SERVES 4–8

Using a sharp knife, cut the top off each pepper and scoop out the seeds and membranes.

To prepare the filling, put the noodles into a bowl, cover with hot water and set aside for 15 minutes. Drain and chop coarsely with kitchen scissors/shears.

Put the peanuts into a frying pan/skillet and dry-toast until aromatic, about 30 seconds. Put into a small blender, add the curry paste, garlic, lime zest and juice, sugar and sesame oil and grind to a paste. Alternatively, use a mortar and pestle.

Stuff the peppers with the peanut mixture, alternately with the noodles, using your fingers to mix the two inside the peppers (do not stuff too tightly). Put the peppers, open-side up, into a small bamboo steamer, then put it inside a larger steamer basket.

Steam over boiling water for about 30 minutes, or until the peppers are tender. Serve in the small steamer, with other Asian dishes.

STEAMED PUMPKIN WITH GARLIC BLACK BEAN SAUCE

A heavy hit of garlic permeates a whole steamed pumpkin in this recipe. The size of the pumpkin and thickness of its flesh will determine how many this serves and how long it takes to steam. It should be tender but not falling apart.

1 small pumpkin
100 g/3½ oz. king oyster mushrooms
2 spring onions/scallions
7 teaspoons crushed/minced garlic
2 tablespoons black bean sauce
2 tablespoons mushroom sauce
100 g/scant ¾ cup pumpkin seeds/pepitas
2 tablespoons sunflower or vegetable oil
fresh coriander/cilantro leaves, to garnish

SERVES 4–8

Core the pumpkin, keeping it whole. Place in a heatproof dish. Set aside.

Slice the mushrooms into 5-mm/¼-in. thick slices, about 6 cm/2¼ in. long. Cut the spring onions/scallions into 6-cm/2¼-in. lengths. Set aside.

Heat the oil in a wok and fry the mushrooms and garlic until fragrant. Add the black bean sauce, mushroom sauce, pumpkin seeds/pepitas and 125 ml/½ cup water, and cook for a few seconds. Lastly, add the spring onions/scallions and give it a quick stir.

Spoon the mixture into the pumpkin core, then place the dish into the steamer basket.

Steam over boiling water for 15–20 minutes until the pumpkin is tender (it will depend on the thickness of the pumpkin; the pumpkin should be soft but still whole). Serve garnished with coriander/cilantro leaves.

STEAMED FLAT RICE NOODLE ROLLS WITH GREEN ASPARAGUS

Flat rice noodle rolls are a classic on dim sum menus, and they are very easily made at home to add to your own Asian spreads.

70 g/generous ½ cup rice flour
10 g/1 tablespoon plus
   1 teaspoon tapioca starch
20 g/3 tablespoons plus
   1 teaspoon cornflour/
   cornstarch
1 tablespoon sunflower or
   vegetable oil
12 asparagus spears, peeled
1 tablespoon black sesame
   seeds, to garnish

SWEET SOY SAUCE
2 teaspoons clear honey
   or sugar
2 tablespoons light soy sauce
2 teaspoons sesame oil

MAKES 18

Put the rice flour, tapioca starch and cornflour/cornstarch into a bowl and add 360 ml/1½ cups water. Whisk until evenly mixed.

Put a heatproof dish into the steamer basket and heat it over rapidly boiling water. Using either dish tongs or heatproof gloves, carefully remove the hot heatproof dish from the steamer basket. Brush the base of the dish with the oil.

Give the mixture a quick stir, then use a ladle to scoop a thin layer of rice flour mixture into the hot dish, tilting the dish so the mixture spreads evenly. Place two asparagus spears along the middle.

Put the dish back into the steamer basket and steam for about 40 seconds over a high heat, or until you see bubbles forming on the flat noodles (it needs to be steaming over rapidly boiling water, otherwise it may take a little longer).

Carefully remove the dish from the basket. Using a flat scraper, gently roll the flat noodle with the asparagus spears in the centre. Cut the noodle roll into three portions.

Repeat the process another five times with the remaining mixture and asparagus spears.

To make the sauce, heat 2 tablespoons water in a small pan and add the honey (or sugar), soy sauce and sesame oil. Stir until dissolved.

Serve the rice noodle rolls with the sauce for diners to add to their liking. Garnish with black sesame seeds.

STEAMED CABBAGE LEAF SPRING ROLLS WITH MIXED VEG FILLING

Savoy cabbage rolls are found across the globe. Whether they are stuffed with Mediterranean ingredients in Italy or, as here, with Asian veggies and flavourings, they are always a delight.

2 carrots

300 g/10½ oz. tung ho leaves (chrysanthemum coronarium)

200 g/7 oz. enoki mushrooms

200 g/7 oz. baby corn

100 g/3½ oz. fresh lotus roots

200 g/7 oz. rice vermicelli, soaked in water for 2 hours

1 tablespoon chopped garlic

2 teaspoons grated fresh ginger

2 tablespoons olive oil, plus extra for brushing

3 tablespoons sesame oil

2 tablespoons soy sauce

2 tablespoons fried shallots

8 Savoy cabbage leaves

salt and freshly ground black pepper

MAKES 8

Julienne the carrots, tung ho leaves and enoki into 6-cm/2¼-in. lengths. Halve the baby corns lengthways. Slice the lotus roots thinly and halve them. Blanch all the veg quickly, then set aside.

Drain the rice vermicelli and place in the steamer basket. Steam the rice vermicelli for 5 minutes over boiling water until softened.

Put the chopped garlic and grated ginger in a small heatproof bowl.

Heat the olive oil in a small pan, pour the hot oil over the bowl of garlic and ginger.

Put the blanched veg and noodles into a bowl and add the sesame oil, soy sauce and fried shallots. Pour in the ginger and garlic mixture and season to taste. Mix well and set aside to cool.

Blanch the Savoy cabbage leaves in boiling water to soften them, the pat them dry and allow to cool.

Arrange the cabbage leaves on the work surface and divide the vegetable and noodle mixture between the leaves. Fold the leaves in from the sides, then roll them into spring rolls. Brush the tops with olive oil.

Place the spring rolls in a round heatproof dish, then place in the steamer basket. Steam for 10 minutes over boiling water, then serve.

THREE TYPES OF STEAMED RICE

Though not technically steaming, the first recipe uses the absorption method – the traditional way of cooking rice in many Asian countries. It's foolproof, and it doesn't seem to matter how much rice you're cooking. The result is light, fluffy and as separate as the variety of rice demands.

Sticky rice, the glutinous variety used in Lao, Thai and Vietnamese cooking, especially for sweet dishes, should always be steamed. Glutinous rice, by the way, does NOT contain gluten.

If you have access to a South-east Asian shop, you may be able to buy the conical woven bamboo rice steamers used in Cambodia. The bamboo, which should be properly soaked before use, is said to give a special flavour to the sticky rice, much appreciated by aficionados.

South-east Asian black rice can be boiled in a saucepan in the usual way (it takes much longer than white rice), but steaming is a traditional method that keeps all the flavours: none disappears into the cooking water. Sometimes, white and black rice are steamed together, and the purple-black colour seeps into the white, giving a beautiful effect.

STEAMED RICE

250 ml/1 cup fragrant Thai rice (see note)

Wash and drain the rice, then put it into a saucepan and add water to one finger's joint above the level of the rice.

Bring to the boil, cover with a lid, reduce the heat to the lowest possible and let steam until done, about 12 minutes.

Let rest, covered, for another 10 minutes.

The rice will be perfectly dry.

STEAMED STICKY RICE

250 ml/1 cup glutinous/sticky rice (see note)

Put the rice into a bowl and rinse, changing the water several times, until the water runs clear. Cover the rice with cold water, put into the fridge and let soak overnight.

When ready to cook, drain the rice, then line a steamer with muslin/cheesecloth or prepare a soaked bamboo steamer (see recipe introduction, above).

Cover and steam for about 45 minutes until done.

Remove from the heat and fluff up with a fork.

STEAMED BLACK RICE

250 ml/1 cup Asian black rice (see note)

Put the rice into a bowl, cover with cold water and let soak for at least 4 hours, or overnight in the fridge.

When ready to cook the rice, drain, then line a steamer with muslin/cheesecloth or prepare a soaked bamboo rice steamer (see recipe introduction, above).

Cover and steam for 1 hour, or until tender. Remove from the heat and fluff up with a fork.

Black rice may also be boiled in a pan for 25–30 minutes, using at least 500 ml/2 cups water.

NOTE Rice should be measured by volume, not weight.
When cooked, the volume increases approximately fourfold.

RICE PARCELS

This is an easy banana leaf version of a more complicated traditional recipe using dried lotus leaves. You can also use a simple foil packet.

4 dried shiitake mushrooms

300 g/1⅓ cups plus
   3 tablespoons jasmine rice

3-cm/1½-in. piece fresh ginger,
   peeled and sliced

2 tablespoons groundnut/
   peanut oil

8 slices smoked bacon,
   sliced crossways

2 eggs

8 pieces banana leaf or dried
   lotus leaf soaked in boiling
   water until supple, or foil,
   20-cm/8-in. square

FLAVOUR MIXTURE

1 tablespoon mirin

1 tablespoon dark soy sauce

1 tablespoon oyster sauce

a pinch sugar

1 teaspoon sesame oil

MAKES 8

Put the mushrooms into a bowl, cover with boiling water and let soak for 30 minutes. Drain, remove and discard the stems and thinly slice the caps.

To make the flavour mixture, put the mirin, soy sauce, oyster sauce, sugar and sesame oil into a bowl, mix well, then set aside.

Put the rice and ginger into a saucepan and add enough water to come one finger's joint above the top of the rice. Bring to the boil, cover and cook for 8 minutes until the rice is part-cooked. Drain and discard the slices of ginger.

Heat the oil in a wok, add the bacon and stir-fry until crisp. Remove and set aside. Put the eggs into a bowl and beat with 1 tablespoon water.

Reheat the bacon fat in the wok and swirl so the sides are well coated, adding a little oil if necessary. Add the beaten eggs and swirl to form a thin omelette. Cook until just set, then roll up the omelette, transfer to a plate and slice thinly.

Put the banana leaf, lotus leaf or foil squares onto a work surface, put 1–2 tablespoons of rice in the centre, then a share of all the other ingredients, including the flavour mixture. Fold up into square parcels, tie with string/twine or secure with cocktail sticks/toothpicks, and set in the steamer basket.

Steam for about 20 minutes, then serve, cutting a cross in the top of each packet just before serving, so the aromas escape across the table.

SWEETS & TREATS

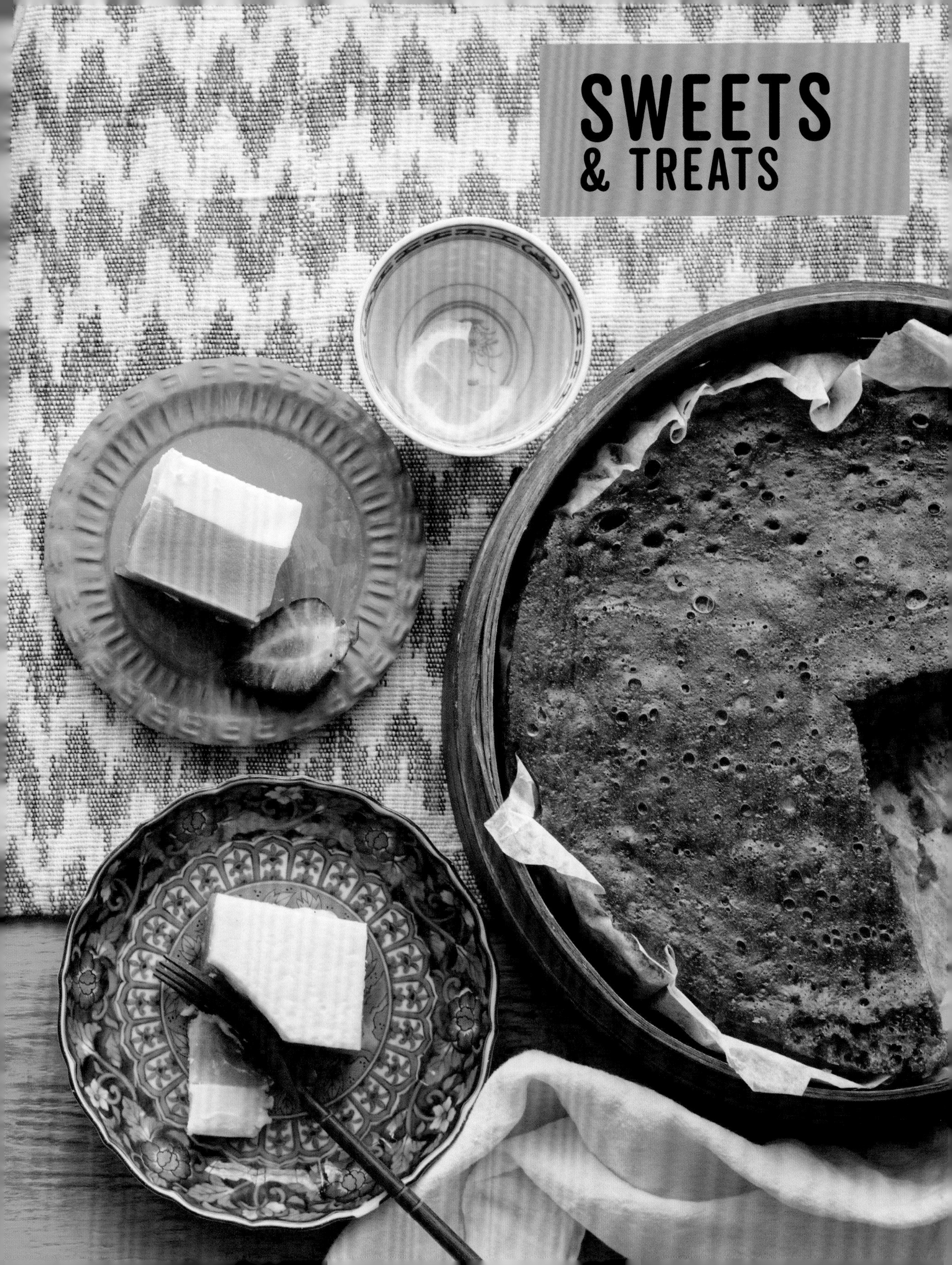

TROPICAL CHILLI/CHILI FRUITS IN PAPER PACKETS

The idea of fresh fruit sprinkled with dried chilli flakes/hot red pepper flakes might seem a bit unusual, but it's a common treat in street markets in India. This recipe is a delicious, easy way to end a meal – heating intensifies the fruit's taste and the dried chilli flakes/hot red pepper flakes give a delicious spark (perfect with sweet things). Remember, you're not cooking the fruit, just warming it to develop the flavours.

2 ripe mangoes

1 ripe papaya

1 ripe banana

1 teaspoon dried chilli flakes/
   hot red pepper flakes,
   or to taste

crème fraîche, to serve

SUGAR LIME SAUCE

4 tablespoons brown sugar
   or palm sugar/jaggery

grated zest and freshly
   squeezed juice of 3 limes

4 tablespoons thick coconut
   cream

SERVES 4

Peel, deseed and cut the mangoes and papaya into short slices or 2-cm/¾-in. cubes. Slice the banana.

To make the sugar lime sauce, put the sugar, lime juice and coconut cream into a small saucepan and simmer until the sugar has dissolved.

Cut four squares of parchment paper or foil, about 30-cm/12-in. square.

Put the fruit in piles in the centre of each square. Sprinkle the sugar lime sauce on top, then sprinkle with the dried chilli flakes/hot red pepper flakes and lime zest.

Close and seal the packets and place in the steamer basket.

Steam over boiling water for 5 minutes, or just until heated through.

Serve in the packets with a separate bowl of crème fraîche.

BLACK RICE WITH RED FRUITS

Black rice in coconut milk is a traditional South-east Asian sweet dish. It is even more delicious teamed with red fruits. For a more tropical taste, feel free to use alternatives, such as papaya or lychees, if you prefer.

210 g/1¼ cups Asian black rice
red fruits, such as cherries or
   raspberries, to serve

COCONUT GINGER SYRUP
500 ml/2 cups coconut cream
4 tablespoons brown sugar
2.5-cm/1-in. piece fresh ginger,
   peeled and grated
salt

SERVES 4

Put the rice into a bowl, cover with cold water and let soak for at least 4 hours, or overnight in the fridge.

When ready to cook the rice, drain, then line a steamer basket with muslin/cheesecloth, or prepare a soaked bamboo rice steamer. Place the rice in the lined steamer basket.

Steam over boiling water for about 1 hour, or until tender. Remove from the heat and fluff up with a fork.

To make the sauce, put the coconut cream into a small saucepan, add the sugar, grated ginger and a pinch of salt. Bring to the boil and cook until the sugar has dissolved.

Add the cooked rice to the pan and simmer until thick. Let cool but do not chill. Once cooled, serve topped with the fruit.

STEAMED CASSAVA CAKE

This South-east-Asian-inspired steamed sweet treat takes a little time to prepare, but is worth the effort. This cake is very soft to eat and hardens in the fridge. It is traditionally eaten with a soft texture, but it can be frozen and steamed to soften again when needed.

1 kg/2 lb. 4 oz. cassava
150 g/¾ cup white sugar
150 ml/⅔ cup coconut milk
8 pandan leaves, halved
1 teaspoon vegetable or
  sunflower oil
400 g/scant 6 cups grated
  coconut (you can buy it frozen
  or grate your own)
salt

2 x 26-cm/10¼-in. cake pans
  (or heatproof dishes), one lined
  with foil

MAKES 10–15

Peel and grate the cassava into a bowl and add 400 ml/scant 1¾ cups water, along with the sugar and coconut milk. Mix it evenly. Pour the mixture into the lined cake pans or heatproof dishes and spread the mixture out evenly.

Arrange half the pandan leaves over the top, then place the pan in the steamer basket.

Steam over boiling water for 40–45 minutes until set.

Place the remaining pandan leaves in the second (unlined) cake pan base.

Mix ½ teaspoon salt into the grated coconut and put into the cake pan on top of the pandan leaves.

Steam the grated coconut over boiling water for 10 minutes (steaming helps to cook the coconut and stop it from going off too quickly). You can do this in a second tier steamer basket, if you like.

Remove the steamed cake and grated coconut from the steamer baskets. Remove and discard all the pandan leaves (they are used as aromatics only and are not to be eaten).

Using a spoon, shape the cake into bite-size pieces, or cut them into rectangles using a sharp knife. Coat each piece of cake with the steamed grated coconut.

MOCHI WITH ADZUKI RED BEAN FILLING

Mochi is a Japanese rice cake, which is made from glutinous/sticky rice flour. The cakes are very soft and chewy, and this version has a sweet-tasting homemade red bean paste filling made from dried adzuki beans.

100 g/¾ cup Thai, Japanese or Korean glutinous/sticky rice flour

50 g/¼ cup unrefined sugar

about 250 g/2½ cups cornflour/cornstarch or potato starch, for dusting

FILLING

200 g/1 cup plus 2 tablespoons dried adzuki red beans, soaked in water overnight

120 g/½ cup plus 2 tablespoons white sugar

30 g/2½ tablespoons soft brown sugar

salt

MAKES 12

For the filling, drain the adzuki red beans and discard the soaking liquid. Put the beans in a pan with 1 litre/4 cups water and bring to the boil. Simmer until softened; check after 1 hour, then again every 30 minutes until the beans are softened.

When the beans are soft, use a wooden spoon to stir in the sugars and 1 teaspoon salt. Continue to stir the beans in the pot until the mixture has almost become a dry paste (stir regularly or the beans can burn easily).

Pass the beans through a fine-mesh sieve/strainer to remove the skins, or you can just leave it as it is.

Allow to cool and then cover and chill in the fridge for at least 2 hours.

Shape the red bean paste into 12 firm balls, then cover and chill again while you make the dough.

Whisk together the glutinuous/sticky rice flour and 150 ml/⅔ cup water in a bowl, then pour into a heatproof dish. Cover the dish with clingfilm/plastic wrap and place into the steamer basket.

Steam over boiling water for 20 minutes, then remove from the steamer, add the sugar, and stir with a wooden spoon until well combined.

Mochi dough is very sticky to work with, so generously dust the work surface and your hands with cornflour/cornstarch.

Roll the mochi dough gently into a long sausage shape, then cut it into 12 portions. Roll each portion into a circle, dusting with cornflour/cornstarch as you go.

Remove the chilled red bean paste from the fridge and place a paste ball on each circle of dough.

Wrap the dough skin round the paste, sealing the seams. Turn the mochi seam-side down and shape it until round.

Dust off excess cornflour/cornstarch before serving.

PANDAN & COCONUT LAYER CAKE

This two-tone layer cake comprises a vibrant green pandan-infused base layer, topped with a brilliant white creamy coconut milk layer – delicious flavours of South-east Asia. Alkaline water is available in large supermarkets.

10 pandan leaves
20 g/¾ oz. mung bean starch
60 g/generous ½ cup tapioca starch
100 g/¾ cup rice flour
140 g/scant ¾ cup white sugar
½ teaspoon alkaline water

COCONUT MILK LAYER
50 g/generous ⅓ cup rice flour
25 g/1 oz. mung bean starch
280 ml/1 cup plus 2 tablespoons thick coconut milk
250 ml/1 cup boiling water
salt

20-cm/8-in. semi-deep heatproof dish, lightly oiled

MAKES 12

Cut the pandan leaves into small pieces and put into a blender with 300 ml/1¼ cups water. Blend until you have pandan juice. Strain through a fine-mesh sieve/strainer to get 300 ml/1¼ cups pandan juice.

Put the mung bean starch, tapioca starch, rice flour and sugar in a bowl. Add the pandan juice, 350 ml/scant 1½ cups water and the alkaline water. Whisk until there are no lumps.

Stain the mixture through a fine-mesh sieve/strainer into a saucepan and set it over a low heat to thicken slightly – it should coat the back of a wooden spoon lightly, do not over cook. Remove from the heat and pour the mixture into the base of the oiled heatproof dish.

Put the dish into the steamer basket and steam over boiling water for 15–20 minutes, or until the mixture is cooked and set.

To prepare the coconut milk layer, mix the rice flour, mung bean starch and 1 teaspoon salt in a heatproof bowl. Add the coconut milk. Gradually add the boiling water whilst whisking until the mixture is smooth. Strain if necessary to get rid of lumps.

Gently pour this layer over the green layer, then steam over boiling water (use a medium heat) for 15–17 minutes, or until the layer is set. It's important not to turn up the heat for this layer or the surface will not be smooth.

Allow the cake to cool completely, which may take an hour or so.

Rub a knife with some oil, or use a plastic knife, to cut the steam cake into small cubes. Wipe the knife with a damp cloth after each cut as the knife will be sticky.

MATCHA MOCHI WITH SWEET POTATO & PUMPKIN FILLING

Another tasty Japanese-inspired mochi recipe, but this time the chewy morsels are coloured green thanks to the matcha powder in the mochi dough, and they are filled with a vibrant orange-coloured sweet potato and pumpkin paste.

100 g/¾ cup Thai, Japanese or Korean glutinous rice flour
5 g/1 teaspoon matcha powder
50 g/¼ cup unrefined sugar
about 250 g/2½ cups cornflour/ cornstarch or potato starch, for dusting

FILLING
150 g/5¼ oz. sweet potato, peeled and chopped
100 g/3½ oz. pumpkin, peeled and chopped
25 g/2 tablespoons caster/ superfine sugar
2 tablespoons sunflower or vegetable oil
50 g/5½ tablespoons pumpkin seeds/pepitas, chopped
salt

MAKES 12

Start by making the filling. Arrange the sweet potato and pumpkin into a heatproof dish and place in the steamer basket. Steam over boiling water for about 20 minutes until softened.

Place the sweet potato and pumpkin into a blender and add the sugar, 60 ml/4 tablespoons water and ⅛ teaspoon salt. Blend until smooth.

Transfer the blended mixture into a frying pan/skillet and add the oil and the chopped pumpkin seeds. Cook over a low heat until the paste is firm.

Allow the paste to cool and then cover and chill in the fridge for at least 2 hours.

Shape the pumpkin paste into 12 balls, then cover and chill again while you make the dough.

Whisk together the glutinuous rice flour, matcha powder and 150 ml/ ⅔ cup water in a bowl, then pour into a heatproof dish. Cover the dish with clingfilm/plastic wrap and place into the steamer basket.

Steam over boiling water for 20 minutes, then remove from the steamer, add the sugar, and stir with a wooden spoon until well combined.

Mochi dough is very sticky to work with, so generously dust the work surface and your hands with cornflour/cornstarch.

Roll the mochi dough gently into a long sausage shape, then cut it into 12 portions. Roll each portion into a circle, dusting with cornflour/ cornstarch as you go.

Remove the chilled sweet potato and pumpkin paste from the fridge and place a paste ball on each circle of dough.

Wrap the dough skin round the paste, sealing the seams. Turn the mochi seam-side down and shape it until round.

Dust off excess cornflour/cornstarch before serving.

BROWN SUGAR SPONGE CAKE

Sweet and treacly, this steamed sponge makes a lovely dessert, or is just as nice served with some tea – green or black, whatever you prefer! You will need two steamer baskets for this recipe; a larger one with a lid, and a smaller one to sit inside it.

3 UK large/US extra-large eggs, at room temperature
120 g/scant ⅔ cup soft brown sugar
160 g/scant 1¼ cups soft white flour
1 tablespoon cornflour/cornstarch
20 g/⅙ cup custard powder/instant vanilla pudding
1 teaspoon easy-bake/rapid-rise dried yeast
150 ml/⅔ cup milk
60 ml/4 tablespoons vegetable oil
1 teaspoon bicarbonate of soda/baking soda
1 teaspoon baking powder
2 teaspoons vanilla paste
30 g/1½ tablespoons black treacle/molasses
salt

23-cm/9-in. bamboo steamer basket, lined with parchment paper
30-cm/12-in. bamboo steamer basket with a lid

SERVES 8

Whisk the eggs in a large bowl until fluffy, then add the soft brown sugar in three parts, whisking it well between each addition. Fold in the soft flour, cornflour/cornstarch, custard powder/instant vanilla pudding and yeast. Lastly, whisk in the milk.

Cover and leave the mixture in a warm room to rest for 2 hours until you see little bubbles at the top.

After 2 hours, fold in the vegetable oil, bicarbonate of soda/baking soda, baking powder, vanilla paste, black treacle/molasses and ½ teaspoon salt. Pour the mixture into the 23-cm/9-in. lined bamboo steamer basket.

Place the 30-cm/12-in bamboo basket over a big pot of boiling water and place the 23-cm/9-in. basket containing the cake mixture inside it. Cover with the lid and steam for 40 minutes until well risen. Do not remove the lid to check it before this time, as the mixture may collapse.

Allow to cool before serving.

STICKY RICE WITH MANGO

In Cambodia, sticky rice is cooked in a woven bamboo basket steamer set over a pot a little like a couscousière. There is a Vietnamese old wives' tale that if you don't look after your stomach, when you get old, you'll have to eat sticky rice – so presumably it's easy to digest.

250 g/1⅓ cups glutinous/sticky
    rice
2 ripe mangoes
250 ml/1 cup coconut milk
4 tablespoons white sugar

salt
freshly grated lime zest,
    to serve

SERVES 4

Put the rice into a bowl and rinse, changing the water several times until the water runs clear. Cover the rice with cold water, put into the fridge and let soak overnight.

When ready to cook, drain the rice, then line a steamer with muslin/cheesecloth or prepare a soaked bamboo steamer.

Cover and steam over boiling water for about 45 minutes until done. Remove from the heat and fluff up with a fork.

Meanwhile, to prepare the mangoes, cut the cheeks off either side of the seed and cut a chequerboard in the flesh without going through the skin. Lift off the diced mango with a fork. Peel the remaining skin off the mango and dice the remaining flesh.

Transfer the cooked rice to a saucepan, add the coconut milk, sugar and a small pinch of salt, and cook until the sugar dissolves and the rice is thick. Serve topped with the mango and sprinkled with lime zest.

NOTE It is traditional to chill the mango, but it has more flavour at room temperature. Also, never put tropical fruit into the fridge for more than 30 minutes or so – you'll give them frostbite!

PEAR & GINGER PUDDINGS

Chinese pears can be found in Chinese supermarkets and specialist greengrocers. They have yellow skin, crisp white flesh and a long black stem. Nashi pears are similar in taste and texture and can be used instead. These puddings are dim-sum-size, but this recipe would make six regular-sized puddings.

100 g/7 tablespoons butter

175 g/½ cup plus 1 tablespoon golden/light corn syrup

3 eggs

225 g/1¾ cups self-raising/self-rising flour, sifted

3 Chinese/nashi pears, peeled, cored and finely chopped, plus extra to decorate

100 g/⅔ cup stem ginger in syrup, finely chopped

12 teacups (see note) or medium ramekins (150 ml/5 fl. oz. each) or 18 small ramekins (100 ml/3½ fl. oz. each), well greased

MAKES 12 MEDIUM OR 18 SMALL

Put the butter and syrup in a large bowl and beat until light and fluffy. Beat in the eggs one at a time. Fold in the flour and then the chopped pears and ginger.

Divide the mixture between the teacups or ramekins in a large bamboo steamer basket (use multiple tiers or cook in batches if necessary).

Set over a wok or saucepan of simmering water and steam for about 30–40 minutes, until cooked, topping up with boiling water as necessary. Serve topped with extra pear slices to decorate.

NOTE To prevent them from cracking in the steamer, teacups should be tempered before use. Put them on a rack in a saucepan and cover with cold water. Cover with a lid, bring to the boil and simmer for 10 minutes. Turn off the heat and let cool to room temperature. The cups are now ready for use.

INDEX

CREDITS

PHOTOGRAPHY
All photography by Clare Winfield with food styling by Flossy McAslan and prop styling by Max Robinson and Lauren Miller, with the exception of the images on pages 2, 3, 16, 27, 28, 40, 46, 48, 54, 57, 58, 62, 65 photography by Louise Hagger, food styling by Emily Kydd and prop styling by Jennifer Kay.

RECIPES
Some recipes in this book were previously published in *Modern Dim Sum* Loretta Liu, *Dim Sum* Fiona Smith, *Steaming* Elsa Petersen-Schepelern and *Vatch's Thai Kitchen* Vatcharin Bhumichitr, as follows.

Loretta Liu
All recipes excluding those listed below.

Elsa Petersen-Schepelern
Pages 44, 75, 76, 79, 84, 92, 95, 96, 99, 100, 103, 104, 107, 108, 119, 120, 127, 135, 136, 140, 143, 155.

Fiona Smith
Pages 51, 52, 60, 68, 71, 72, 88, 91, 123, 156.

Vatcharin Bhumichitr
Pages 80, 83.